The Adaptive Organization

A Darwinian Approach to Management

ADA WALLACE

CONTENTS

WHY I WROTE THIS BOOK

I am an ecologist who has been doing research on evolutionary processes for over 25 years. Viewed through the lens of evolution, it is pretty apparent why some companies succeed while others fail. In today's rapidly changing business climate it is not a winning strategy to be stationary. As in nature, the secret to success is constant **adaptation** to the circumstances.

But writing management literature is not the path to success for a scientist, so I write this under pseudonym. I have borrowed my last name from Alfred Russel Wallace, who discovered natural selection at the same time as Darwin. It was Wallace who coined the term "Darwinism". He is well known among biologists, just not to the general public. I have borrowed my first name from Ada Lovelace, the first programmer. Further, I have used AI to rephrase my style of writing, to a style more suited to management literature.

The tricks to adaptation are well known in evolutionary biology. Scientists have been studying this process since its discovery in the 19th century. Research has been especially productive since the discovery of Mendelian genetic inheritance and the ensuing Modern Synthesis of evolutionary biology. Don't worry if you don't know these terms, they will not be necessary for understanding the book. On the contrary, I have gone to great lengths to ensure that this book is written using the same language as other management literature. But rest assured, the reasoning is scientific.

- **A fresh perspective**. The book presents a fresh and innovative approach to management by applying Darwinian principles. These are based on knowledge gained from scientific research on evolutionary processes.

- **Practical strategies and tactics**. In the book, I provide practical strategies and tactics for implementing the Darwinian approach to management in a real-world context, making it useful for professionals looking to implement change within their organization.

- **Simple language and enthusiastic tone**. I aim to present the information in a simple, pedagogic language and with an enthusiastic tone, aiming to make the book an engaging and enjoyable read for management professionals.

- **Emphasis on resilience and continuous learning**. The book emphasizes the importance of resilience and continuous learning in the business world, providing valuable insights on the value of experimentation and suggests best practices for organizations facing challenges in a rapidly changing business environment.

- **The combination of science and management**. By combining the principles of science and management, the book provides a unique and compelling perspective on the challenges and opportunities faced by organizations in a rapidly changing business environment.

This sets the book apart from other management literature and makes it a valuable resource for professionals seeking to stay ahead of the curve.

1 CALL TO ACTION: AN INTRODUCTION TO THE ADAPTIVE ORGANIZATION

In today's rapidly changing business environment, companies face a multitude of challenges that require innovative and adaptive solutions. Traditional management styles do not adequately satisfy the demands of this new economic landscape. Companies must embrace new ways of thinking and conducting business to be competitive and flourish in an ever-developing marketplace.

This is where the Darwinian approach to management comes in. Inspired by the principles of evolution, it views the corporate world as an ecosystem in which organizations must adapt and develop in order to live and prosper. By embracing change and experimentation, companies can build resilience and agility, and become more adaptive to the challenges of the modern business environment.

In this book, we will look at the advantages of taking a Darwinian approach to management and present a road map for firms wishing to make the switch. We will look at the main components of an adaptive organizational culture, the role of leadership in directing change, and tactics for overcoming opposition and managing transformational hurdles.

The objective is to provide a scientifically based guide to management that is accessible and easy to understand. At the end of this book, you will have a better knowledge of the Darwinian management approach and the skills required to construct an adaptive organization. The book is well suited for both corporate and departmental management.

The Adaptive Organization. A Darwinian Approach to Management is an in-depth look at a new approach of managing. We will investigate the following themes and objectives.

- **The science of evolution and its applications for management.** A look at the advantages of using a Darwinian approach to management, such as enhanced resilience, agility, and adaptability.
- **Overcoming change resistance.** Tactics for gaining stakeholder buy-in and overcoming opposition to guarantee a seamless transition to a Darwinian strategy.
- **Creating an adaptive culture.** Overview of how leadership shapes organizational culture and creates a feeling of shared purpose.
- **Embracing experimentation and failure.** Ways of overcoming failure anxiety and embracing a development mentality.
- **Leading with resilience.** The importance of leadership in dealing with adversity and change, as well as the qualities of resilient leaders.
- **Assessing and enhancing performance.** The crucial aspect of performance evaluation and improvement methodologies, as well as the significance of continuous improvement in developing an adaptable organization.

By delving into these themes and aims, I intend to give a complete reference to the Darwinian management style and empower readers with the information and skills they need to establish an adaptable company.

What this book is not. Through popular accounts of evolution it may sometimes seems as "the survival of the fittest" means "the survival of the strongest". It does not. Evolution is not the tale of stronger individuals replacing the weak. What "the fittest" means differs according to circumstance. Sometimes it is the most caretaking, other times the smartest, the least energy consuming, the most beautiful, the least conspicuous, and so on. Only sometimes is winning the Darwinian race about strength.

The secret to Darwinian management is not to be the strongest but to be the most adaptable. This is the crucial lesson of this book. But don't stop reading just yet – there is more. Because how, exactly, does a company become more adaptable?

That evolutionary success is not about strength is especially true when it comes to humans. It's not because human have particularly dominant alpha males who rule over the alpha males of other species that humans have colonized the globe at the expense of other species. Just look at the competition on the savannah and compare us to it. It would be plain stupid to try to kill a lion alone with traditional weapons, to go head-to-head with an African buffalo alone, or even to single handedly take on a warthog. And stupid we are not (at least not compared to other animals). It takes a *team* to kill a lion.

The secret to human success is cooperation. And that is the situation managers are in. You must create the best and most adaptable *teams* if you want to win in a market that is changing quickly.

Darwinian management is *not* about letting employees battle it out and weed out the weak. Darwinian management focuses on maximizing each person's strengths for the benefit of the team. Don't step on people on the way to success. Besides making you an asshole, it is also bad business.

Companies face competitors, threats, and opportunities every day, and those that were once leaders in their industries may quickly find themselves struggling to remain relevant. Many corporations will periodically end up at a crossroads and must make critical decisions to secure future success. With high stakes and the future of the company on the line, this is the time for action.

As the world continues to change, corporations face challenges and obstacles never encountered before, and struggle to remain competitive. To remain relevant and succeed, companies must be willing to adapt to constant change.

The Darwinian approach to management is a scientifically based, evolution-inspired framework that emphasizes adaptability and resilience in the face of change. The approach is built on the principles of natural selection and evolution, and it provides a way for organizations to navigate the challenges of an ever-shifting business environment. In this book, the reader will gain a clear understanding of what the Darwinian approach is, and why it is so well-suited to such challenges.

What is the Darwinian approach to management?

- The Darwinian approach to management is a management philosophy that draws inspiration from the theory of evolution. The approach emphasizes adaptability and evolution in the business world, and views organizations as dynamic systems that must continuously adapt and evolve to survive and thrive in a rapidly changing environment.

- The Darwinian approach to management recognizes that the business environment is constantly changing and that organizations must be able to change and evolve in response to new challenges to be successful. It encourages organizations to be proactive, innovative, and adaptive, and to continuously improve through experimentation and learning.

- The Darwinian approach to management places a strong emphasis on the role of leadership in facilitating organizational change and guiding the organization towards success. Leaders are seen as key players in promoting a culture of adaptability and continuous improvement, and in helping the organization to evolve and grow.

- The Darwinian approach to management provides a framework for organizations to thrive, by embracing the principle of adaptability and continuously improving through experimentation and learning.

Good and bad examples. Amazon, Netflix, Google, Tesla, and Spotify all made good management decisions from a Darwinian perspective. These companies were willing to experiment with new business models and embrace new technologies. They were quick to respond to changes in their respective industries. They also placed a strong focus on the customer, gathering data on customer preferences and behaviors to inform their product development and business strategy.

On the other hand, Kodak, Blockbuster, Sears, Blackberry, and Borders all had shortcomings from a Darwinian perspective. These companies were *not* willing to experiment with new business models or embrace new technologies. They were slow to respond to changes in their respective industries. They also lacked a focus on the customer and were not willing to gather data on customer preferences and behaviors, which ultimately led to their decline and eventual failure. Failing to adapt to rapidly changing market conditions meant that they were unable to keep pace with their competitors. Their lack of innovation and willingness to embrace change were key factors in their downfall.

Darwinian theory. Darwinian theory is rooted in the principles of evolution and natural selection, which describe how species change and adapt over time in response to their environment. In the same way, businesses can change and adapt over time to remain competitive and successful in the marketplace. Here follow some key principles of Darwinian theory.

- **Variation** refers to the different traits that exist among individuals within a species. In business, variation refers to the differences that exist among employees, teams, and departments. This variation is a crucial component of business adaptability, as it allows organizations to more quickly identify and capitalize on new opportunities.

- **Inheritance** refers to the passing down of traits from one generation to the next. In business, inheritance refers to the passing down of skills, knowledge, and expertise from one generation of employees to the next. This helps to ensure that valuable company knowledge and skills are not lost over time.

- **Selection** refers to the process by which certain traits are passed on to the next generation, while others are not. In business, selection refers to the process by which certain employees, teams, and departments are chosen to take on new projects or responsibilities, while others are not. This process helps to ensure that resources are allocated in the most efficient and effective way possible.

- **Adaptation** refers to the process by which species change over time to better fit their environment. In business, adaptation refers to the process by which organizations change over time to better fit their market, customers, and competition. This is the key to business success, as it allows organizations to remain competitive and relevant in an ever-changing marketplace.

By understanding these key principles of Darwinian theory, organizations can begin to understand how to apply them to their business operations to build a more adaptive, resilient, and successful organization.

A crucial point, that bears repeating, is that the business world is constantly changing. Companies must adapt to stay ahead of the curve. From shifting market trends to new technologies, it can be difficult for companies to stay ahead of the competition and maintain their position in the market. In this context, traditional management practices may no longer be sufficient, and a new approach is needed to navigate these challenges and achieve success.

The Darwinian approach encourages organizations to be more adaptable and resilient in the face of change. This approach to management places a strong emphasis on the importance of experimentation, observation, and adaptation. Just as species in nature must continuously adapt to changing environments to survive and thrive, organizations must be able to adapt to the changing business environment to remain relevant and competitive. The approach recognizes that there is no one-size-fits-all solution and encourages organizations to be flexible and creative. By encouraging and facilitating employees to think creatively and embrace new ideas, organizations can stay ahead of the curve and maintain a competitive advantage.

By valuing different perspectives and encouraging interdepartmental cooperation, organizations can leverage the strengths of all their employees and achieve greater success. Just as a variation increases chances of survival in nature, a diverse range of perspectives and ideas within an organization will lead to more innovative solutions and improved decision-making. By fostering a culture of collaboration, organizations can take advantage of the strengths of all their employees and achieve greater success.

To survive, organizations must compete for customers, funding, and market share. The organizations that are best able to adapt and evolve in response to changes in the market are more likely to survive and succeed. Adopting a Darwinian approach to management can bring numerous benefits to an organization. By promoting adaptability, innovation, collaboration, and informed decision-making, organizations can thrive and succeed.

Darwinian principles, inspired by natural selection, provides a new and innovative approach to management. By adopting a Darwinian mindset, organizations can become more agile, innovative, and capable of thriving in a rapidly changing business environment. This book is to introduces the Darwinian approach to management and provides practical strategies and tactics for organizations seeking to embrace this new way of thinking.

Are you willing and able to take the leap?

2 OVERCOMING RESISTANCE TO CHANGE

Before we can dive into the topic at hand, we must first deal with the problem of resistance. Not everyone embraces continuous change. Not everyone welcomes new thinking. Not everyone is open to scientific approaches. Change is inevitable nevertheless, but you need to be aware that not everyone welcomes change with open arms. Sitting still is comfortable. Exploring new ideas is more challenging.

When it comes to organizational change, it's common that co-workers – both managers and employees – resist change. Resistance to change can manifest in many forms, from passively ignoring new directives to actively opposing them. This section will examine what resistance to change is about and why it happens.

Resistance to change is a natural response to new and unknown situations. People tend to cling to what they know and what has worked in the past, and change can threaten that comfort and stability. "Don't change what isn't broken" as the saying goes. But then you will inevitably be overtaken by market competitors. Resistance can stem from factors such as fear of the unknown, concerns about job security, and from lack of trust in the motives behind the change.

But be aware that resistance to change is not necessarily a bad thing. In some cases, it can highlight valid concerns that need to be addressed before a change can be successfully implemented. When resistance goes unaddressed, it can undermine the change process and cause delays, or even derail the entire process.

To overcome resistance to change, it is important to understand its root causes. In many cases, resistance is not a direct opposition to the change itself, but rather a manifestation of underlying fears and concerns. For example, employees may resist change because they are afraid of losing their job or because they don't understand the benefits of the new approach. By understanding the root causes of resistance, organizations can address these concerns and reduce resistance.

Change can be difficult, especially in established organizations where people are comfortable with the way things are. When proposing a new approach to management, it's not uncommon to encounter resistance from those who are hesitant to leave behind familiar practices and embrace something new. However, the success of an organization depends on its ability to adapt and evolve, and the benefits of a Darwinian approach to management are significant.

Common sources of resistance. Resistance to change can come from sources both internal and external to the organization. Some common sources of resistance include lack of trust, fear of the unknown, inertia, personal investment, and lack of understanding. What are the specific sources of resistance in your organization? By identifying these, you can tailor your approach to overcoming resistance and successfully implement the desired changes.

- **Lack of trust**. If your co-workers don't trust the motives behind the change, they are more likely to resist. This can stem from past experiences with less successful change or a lack of transparency in the change process. Make your motives clear: change is about survival and creating a thriving organization.
- **Fear of the unknown**. Change can be frightening, especially when the outcome is uncertain – which it always is. Co-workers may resist change because they are afraid of what the future may hold and how it will affect their job security. Clarify your vision for the future and why it is appealing. Explain the importance of constant development.

- **Inertia**. People often resist change because they are comfortable with the status quo and don't see a compelling reason to change. This can be especially true for long-time employees who are used to the current way of doing things. But standing still in a rapidly changing business environment is dangerous and may lead to the demise of the company.

- **Personal investment**. Co-workers may resist change because they have invested a lot of time and energy into the current system or processes and don't want to start from scratch. Celebrate past contributions, but never let it stand in the way of improvement.

- **Lack of understanding**. Sometimes resistance to change stems from a lack of understanding about what is being proposed. Clear and effective communication can help overcome this type of resistance. Always be transparent about methods and goals.

- **Concerns about the impact on job security**. Employees may be concerned that the new approach may lead to job loss or downsizing. However, ultimately it is company survival that the Darwinian approach is about.

Potential consequences of resistance. Resistance to change can have significant consequences for an organization if it goes unaddressed. It's important to understand the consequences of resistance so that you can take proactive steps to address and overcome them. Some common consequences of resistance include.

- **Delays in implementation**. If resistance is strong, it can slow down or even halt the change process, causing delays in the implementation of the new changes.

- **Increased costs**. Resistance can be time-consuming and resource intensive. The longer it takes to implement changes, the higher the costs will be.

- **Decreased morale**. Resistance to change can cause frustration and decreased morale.

- **Decreased productivity.** When employees resist change, it can lead to decreased productivity as they struggle to adapt to the new way of doing things.
- **Loss of credibility.** If resistance to change is not effectively addressed, it can damage the credibility of the leadership team and the organization as a whole.

The benefits and rewards of embracing change. Embracing change can bring many benefits and rewards for both the organization and its employees. Here are some of the key benefits of embracing change.

- **Innovation.** Embracing change can lead to innovation and new ideas that improve the way the organization operates. This helps the organization stay ahead of the competiti on and achieve long-term success.
- **Increased Productivity.** By embracing change and improving processes, organizations can increase their productivity and efficiency. This leads to cost savings and improved performance.
- **Employee Engagement.** When employees are involved in the change process and see the benefits of the change, they are more likely to be engaged and committed to the organization. This leads to increased job satisfaction and reduced turnover.
- **Improved Adaptability.** Embracing change helps organizations become more adaptable and flexible. This is especially important in today's rapidly changing business environment where organizations need to be able to respond quickly to new challenges and opportunities.
- **Increased Resilience.** By embracing change, organizations become more resilient and better equipped to handle challenges and obstacles. This helps organizations weather economic downturns and other difficult times.

Strategies and approaches to overcome resistance. Resistance to change is a natural and common phenomenon in organizations. It is important to overcome this resistance to successfully implement a new approach to management. Here are some strategies and approaches that can help overcome resistance to change. By using these strategies and approaches, leaders can effectively overcome resistance to change and successfully implement a new approach to management.

- **Communication**. Effective communication is key. Leaders should clearly communicate the reasons for the change, the benefits it will bring, and how it will affect the organization. This can help employees understand the change and feel more confident about it.

- **Involvement**. By giving co-workers a sense of ownership and control, employees are more likely to embrace change. This can be done through involving employees in decision making, providing training and support, and seeking their feedback and input.

- **Addressing concerns**. It's important to listen to and address the concerns of employees who are resistant to change. By addressing their concerns, leaders can help employees feel more comfortable with the change and reduce their resistance.

- **Lead by example**. Leaders must lead by example and demonstrate their commitment to the change. This can help build trust and credibility with employees and encourage them to embrace the change.

- **Celebrates successes**. Celebrating successes along the way can help overcome resistance to change. By showing employees the benefits of the change, leaders can help employees feel more positive about it and reduce their resistance.

The solution to overcoming resistance is to work together.
Throughout this process, remember that the human superpower is cooperation. By giving employees a sense of ownership and responsibility, they are more likely to embrace the new approach and become champions of the change.

If nothing else works, do not shun the option to involve external experts and advisors. Bringing in experts who have experience with the Darwinian approach provides valuable insights and help to build confidence in the new approach. These experts also serve as a resource for employees, providing guidance and support as they navigate the change process.

It's also important to communicate regularly and transparently about the progress of the change. Regular updates help to build trust and keep employees informed about what is happening, what the goals are, and how the change is affecting the organization. This also helps to dispel any rumors or misunderstandings that may arise.

Finally, organizations must be willing and able to listen to feedback and make changes as needed. The adaptive nature of the Darwinian approach means that it should be adjusted and improved as needed. It is important to remain flexible and open to feedback. This ensures that the new approach is effective and sustainable over the long term.

Explain and educate. Employee education on the advantages of the Darwinian management style is one efficient strategy to lower resistance. Explaining how the new strategy will boost the company's competitiveness, how it will help employees, and how it will improve the working environment are some examples of what this can entail. This teaching ought to be followed by succinct communications that highlights the advantages of the new strategy.

It's crucial to convey the dangers of staying the same. Organizations can highlight the potential repercussions of failing to adapt to a business environment that is fast changing and boost buy-in by doing so. Explaining the dangers of falling behind competitors, the possibility of lower profitability, and the effects on employee morale and job security are a few examples of what this can entail.

Give workers a detailed vision of the future. Organizations can create enthusiasm and expectation for the future by describing how the firm will appear when the change has been executed. This may aid in lowering opposition and boosting support for the novel strategy.

Employee worries and concerns should be acknowledged and addressed. Organizations can increase trust and credibility and lessen resistance to change by understanding these worries and responding to them thoughtfully and sympathetically.

Employee involvement in the transformation process helps foster ownership and buy-in. Employers can tap into the workforce's collective intelligence and creativity to develop and implement the new strategy while also lowering resistance to change.

Another potentially important strategy to demonstrate the advantages of the new technique is to trial it first on a modest scale before implementing it more widely. This can assist firms in testing the new strategy in a controlled setting and in identifying and resolving any potential problems or hurdles. Organizations can enhance support for the change and lower resistance by piloting the new strategy.

Companies should also provide staff with training and assistance as they adjust to the new strategy. This can entail granting access to materials and equipment, presenting workshops and training sessions, and supplying one-on-one help as required. Organizations may assist employees in gaining the abilities and knowledge necessary for success as well as lower change resistance by providing this support.

Recognizing and rewarding employees for their efforts and accomplishments is also crucial. Organizations can create a good, encouraging culture that welcomes change and evolution by praising and rewarding people for their commitment and hard work. This may lessen employees' reluctance to change and inspire them to keep coming up with new ideas and strategies to adapt to the company environment's constant change.

It is essential to have support from all relevant parties, including employees, senior management, and important decision-makers, to successfully execute the Darwinian approach to management. These are some explanations for why buy-in is crucial.

- **A higher chance of success**. The likelihood of success rises when stakeholders are on board with the new strategy since they are more likely to accept the changes and support their execution.

- **A rise in morale**. Employees are more likely to be engaged and motivated in their work, improving morale and job satisfaction, when they feel heard and included in the change process.
- **Greater support**. The likelihood that important stakeholders will contribute resources, support, and direction for the new approach's effective adoption increases when they are in favor of it.
- **Increased accountability**. Stakeholders are more likely to be accountable for their actions and duties in implementing the new method when they have a stake in its success.
- **Better decision-making**. Stakeholder buy-in increases the possibility that well-informed decisions will be made since they have a deeper understanding of the new approach's guiding concepts and objectives.

3 GUIDED BY SCIENCE:
HOW EVOLUTION INFORMS MANAGEMENT

The science of evolution provides a powerful framework for understanding the process of change and adaptation. At its core, evolution is about the survival of the fittest, the idea that the species or individuals best adapted to their environment will thrive and reproduce. In the business world, this concept can be applied to companies that are able to adapt and change to meet the demands of a rapidly changing environment.

Just as species must experiment with new behaviors and traits to survive, companies must experiment with new products, processes, and strategies to stay ahead of the curve. Evolution is driven by selection, the process by which certain traits and behaviors are passed on to future generations because they are beneficial. In the business world, this is reflected in the process of market selection, where the companies that can offer the most value to customers will succeed and grow.

Change need not always be gradual and incremental. Sometimes, sudden and disruptive events, such as environmental changes or technological advancements, can trigger rapid and dramatic changes in species. In the business world, these disruptive events can take the form of new competitors, changing consumer preferences, or breakthrough technologies.

In this chapter, we will explore the implications of these and other principles of evolution for management and leadership. By understanding the process of evolution, we can better understand the process of change and adaptation in the business world and develop strategies for leading companies and organizations through this process. The Darwinian approach to management recognizes that change is constant and inevitable, and that companies must be able to adapt and evolve to survive and thrive.

Experimentation, innovation, and failure. One of the key elements of the Darwinian approach is the emphasis on experimentation and innovation. To succeed, companies must be willing to take risks, try new things, experiment with new ideas, products, processes, and embrace failure. Failures should not be shunned but constitute opportunities to learn and grow. Experimentation helps organizations to identify new opportunities and to stay ahead of the curve. This requires both a leadership that is ready to take calculated risks and promote new ideas, as well as a culture that values and encourages risk-taking.

Experimentation is not just about developing new products or services. It can also be about testing new processes, organizational structures, or business models. The key is to create an environment where it is safe to experiment, where employees feel encouraged to come up with new ideas and where management is willing to take calculated risks.

One method to encourage experimentation is to set up a dedicated innovation lab, where employees can work on new ideas and projects in a supportive and collaborative environment. Another approach is to establish a culture of continuous improvement, where employees are encouraged to suggest ways to improve processes and procedures on an ongoing basis.

However, it is important to accept that not all experiments will be successful. Some fail, many may not produce expected results. The key to adaptation is to embrace these failures as opportunities to learn and improve, rather than seeing them as setbacks or disappointments. In the Darwinian approach, failure is a necessary and natural part of the process of change and adaptation. Failure is a necessary part of the journey towards success.

Selection and adaptation. Another important aspect of the Darwinian approach is the focus on selection and adaptation. Companies must continuously select ideas, products, and processes to adapt to changing needs of their customers and the market. This requires a flexible and agile organization, one that can quickly pivot and change course in response to changing circumstances.

Selection is the process of identifying the best ideas, products, and processes and bringing them to market. This requires a culture that supports collaboration and cross-functional teamwork, as well as a leadership that can make difficult decisions and prioritize the most promising opportunities.

Adaptation is about being able to change course quickly and effectively in response to changing circumstances. This requires an organization that can respond quickly to new information, and to make decisions and take actions in a timely and efficient manner.

Leadership. Darwinian leaders must be able to envision and guide the company through the process of change and adaptation. This requires a combination of creativity, vision, and determination, as well as the ability to identify navigate obstacles and challenges that arise along the way.

Leadership in a Darwinian organization requires a combination of creativity, vision, and determination, as well as the ability to make tough decisions and to take calculated risks. Leaders must also be able to inspire and motivate their employees, and to create a culture that supports collaboration and teamwork.

The Darwinian approach to management provides a powerful framework for understanding the process of change and adaptation in the business world. By embracing experimentation and innovation, focusing on selection and adaptation, and providing strong and visionary leadership, companies can succeed.

Scientific background

The theory of evolution refers to two things. First, it is about the history of life on earth. Second, it is the scientific explanation for the process by which species of living organisms change over time through the mechanism of natural selection. It is this latter part that was novel in Darwin's theory and what can be used to inform management practices. The theory was first presented comprehensively by Charles Darwin in his book *On the Origin of Species* published in 1859.

Darwin described how populations of organisms are subject to variation, with some individuals having traits that are better suited to their environment than others. These individuals are more likely to survive and reproduce, passing on their advantageous traits to their offspring. Over time, this gradual process of natural selection results in changes to the populations, leading to the development of new species and adaptations to the environment.

The theory of evolution is widely accepted by the scientific community and has been supported by an immense body of evidence from fields such as biology, paleontology, genetics, and anthropology. It is considered one of the most important scientific theories that exist and a necessary framework for understanding the diversity of life on Earth, adaptations of living species, and the process of how species have changed over time.

Natural selection. Natural selection is the process by which certain traits and characteristics become more prevalent in a population over time because they provide a survival advantage. This occurs as individuals with advantageous traits are more likely to survive and reproduce, passing on those traits to their offspring. Over generations, the proportion of individuals with the advantageous traits increases, leading to the evolution of new species and adaptations.

Natural selection acts on the variation that exists within a population. This variation can result from mutations, genetic recombination, and other processes. Some of these variations are beneficial and provide a survival advantage, while others are neutral or harmful. The beneficial traits are more likely to be passed on to future generations, while the harmful traits are less likely to be passed on. Over time, this process leads to the evolution of a population, as the frequency of advantageous traits increases.

The theory of natural selection is one of the central mechanisms by which evolution occurs. It provides a way to understand how species change and adapt over time in response to environmental pressures and other factors.

Sexual selection. Sexual selection is a special case of natural selection that refers to how certain traits or behaviors evolve as a result of an individual's ability to attract or compete for mates. Unlike natural selection, which focuses on an organism's ability to survive and reproduce, sexual selection focuses on the role of mating preferences and the evolution of traits that enhance an individual's ability to mate successfully.

Sexual selection operates through two mechanisms. *intersexual* selection and *intrasexual* selection. Intersexual selection occurs when members of one sex choose mates based on certain traits, such as appearance, coloration, or behavior. Over time, these mating preferences can drive the evolution of these traits. Intrasexual selection, on the other hand, refers to competition among individuals of the same sex for access to mates. This can result in the evolution of traits that allow individuals to physically dominate or defeat their rivals, such as size, strength, or aggression.

Sexual selection can result in the evolution of exaggerated or costly traits, such as large antlers in male deer or bright plumage in birds, that may have little or no impact on survival but serve as an indicator of good genes or an individual's ability to compete for mates. (Weaponry, such as antlers in deer, did most often not evolve as defensive weapons against predators, but as offensive weapons used against competitors.) Over time, these traits can become more exaggerated as they are favored by sexual selection and can come to be seen as hallmarks of the species.

How natural and sexual selection apply to business management. The theory of evolution and the processes of natural selection and sexual selection can be applied to business management in several ways.

In terms of natural selection, businesses must evolve and adapt to changing conditions to survive and thrive. This means continuously evaluating their products, practices and processes, and making changes necessary to stay ahead of the competition and meet the needs of their customers.

In terms of sexual selection, just as peacocks with elaborate feathers are more attractive to female peahens, individuals with certain characteristics may be more attractive to employers or colleagues. These characteristics can include traits such as confidence, charisma, assertiveness, social skills, or physical attractiveness.

Also, just as certain physical traits can signal good health or genetic fitness in the animal kingdom, certain professional accomplishments, such as awards, degrees, or successful projects, can signal competence or potential for success in the workplace.

Beware, however, that applying the concept of sexual selection to business management often should be used more as a warning. While certain personal traits may be individually advantageous, a successful career that also is beneficial to a company above all requires hard work, skill, and dedication. Also, applying sexual selection principles in a professional setting can raise ethical concerns and risks perpetuating discriminatory practices.

Darwinian management practices are so powerful that they need to be applied with great skill and care. The principles of evolution, natural selection, and sexual selection can help organizations understand the importance of constantly adapting and evolving.

Inheritance in the evolutionary process. Inheritance is a fundamental concept in evolutionary biology and refers to the transmission of traits from one generation to the next. Inheritance plays a crucial role in the evolutionary process because it is the mechanism through which genetic variation is passed from one generation to the next, providing the raw material for natural selection to act upon.

Inheritance occurs when genetic material, in the form of DNA, is passed from parents to offspring. This DNA contains the instructions for building and maintaining an organism, and it also contains the variation that is the source of diversity within species. This variation can be beneficial, neutral, or harmful. Natural selection acts on this variation, favoring traits that increase the likelihood of survival and reproduction. Inheritance also plays a role in sexual selection, as the traits that are attractive to mates are often passed down to offspring. Over time, this can result in the evolution of traits that are attractive but have no real benefit to survival, such as the bright feathers of many birds.

In the context of business management, inheritance can be thought of as the passing on of organizational culture, knowledge, skills, and processes from one generation of employees to the next. It is crucial to remember what works and to pass it on. And just as inheritance plays a crucial role in the evolutionary process by providing the raw material for natural selection to act upon, the inheritance of organizational culture and knowledge provides the foundation for the continued growth and success of an organization. By passing on best practices, processes, and knowledge that have helped the organization succeed in the past, the organization can ensure its continued evolution and adaptation to changing conditions in the future.

The role of variation in the evolutionary process. Variation plays a crucial role in the evolutionary process. Evolution occurs because of changes in the genetic makeup of a population over time. Variation that is selected can arise from mutations, recombination of genes, or other processes.

The presence of variation in a population provides the raw material for evolution to act upon. For example, in the process of natural selection, individuals with variations that are advantageous in their environment are more likely to survive and pass on those beneficial traits to their offspring. Over time, if these advantageous traits continue to be favored by the environment, they can become more common in the population and lead to the evolution of new species or adaptations.

In the same way, variation in a business organization can also lead to evolution and adaptation. For example, if a company has a culture of innovation and encourages employees to bring new ideas and approaches to the table, it is more likely to evolve and adapt to changing market conditions and customer needs. Similarly, the presence of diverse perspectives and skill sets among employees can lead to the development of new products and services, increased competitiveness, and overall success for the organization.

Selection in the evolutionary process. Selection is the process in evolution where certain traits and characteristics are favored over others based on their ability to provide an advantage in a given environment. The role of selection in the evolutionary process is critical because it determines which traits will be passed down to future generations. Selection acts as a driving force in evolution, allowing species to adapt to their environment and overcome challenges.

In the context of business management, selection refers to the process of choosing certain ideas, products, organization structures, or processes over others based on their perceived fitness or suitability to the organization's goals and needs. This is similar to the process of natural selection, where certain traits and behaviors are selected over others because they provide an advantage in the current environment, allowing individuals to better survive and reproduce. In a business setting, selection may occur in various ways, including but not limited to.

1. **Employee selection**. Choosing and rewarding employees who have the necessary skills and qualifications to perform well in a particular role, and who align with the organization's values and culture.

2. **Idea selection**. Evaluating different ideas and strategies for achieving goals and choosing those that are most likely to succeed based on data and past experience.

3. **Product selection**. Evaluating different products or services to determine which ones are most likely to sell well, meet customer needs, and be profitable for the organization.

4. **Process selection**. Evaluating different processes for achieving goals and choosing those that are most efficient and effective.

The process of selection is critical in helping organizations to evolve and adapt to changing circumstances, just as natural selection helps species to evolve and adapt to changing environments.

Adaptation. Over time, traits that are most advantageous for survival and reproduction become more common in the population, while traits that are less advantageous become less common. This is because organisms with advantageous traits are more likely to survive and reproduce, passing those traits on to their offspring. Through this process of natural selection, populations of organisms gradually change and evolve over time. Adaptation is a key factor in the survival and evolution of species and plays a crucial role in shaping the characteristics and diversity of life on Earth.

In the context of business management, adaptation refers to the process of adjusting and modifying products, organizational practices, processes, and structures in response to changes in the internal and external environment. Adaptation allows organizations to remain competitive, flexible, and resilient in a constantly evolving business landscape.

In an adaptive organization, management recognizes that change is inevitable and proactively implements strategies to respond to changes and challenges in an effective and efficient manner. This requires a culture that values continuous improvement, encourages risk-taking and experimentation, and fosters a learning-oriented mindset among employees.

The role of selection in management evolutionary processes refers to the process of choosing which strategies and practices to adopt, modify, or discard in response to changes in the environment. Managers must carefully evaluate and assess the effectiveness of different practices and make informed decisions about which ones to continue or change.

Ultimately, the goal of adaptation in management is to create a resilient and adaptive organization that can continuously evolve and improve over time, adapting to the changing needs of its customers, employees, and stakeholders, and achieving sustainable success.

4 OUT OF THE COMFORT ZONE: BUILDING AN ADAPTIVE CULTURE

This chapter will begin with a brief outline of the importance of your personal development in learning to challenge yourself and moving above and beyond your normal working processes. It will then continue to the question of how the company should embrace experimentation and failure.

Personal development

Your comfort zone is the familiar and predictable environment where you feel safe and secure. While it can provide a sense of stability and security, it can also limit your growth and potential. To achieve success, if you want to drive improvement you must be willing to step out of your comfort zone and embrace change. Stepping out of your comfort zone brings a variety of benefits, not only for the company but for you personally.

- **Personal growth**. By taking risks and embracing new experiences, you expand your horizons and grow as a person. Besides new skills and knowledge, you gain a fresh perspective on your abilities and potential.
- **Skill development**. By taking on new challenges and responsibilities, you develop new skills and knowledge that will serve you well in future endeavors. This can include everything from technical skills to leadership and communication skills.

- **Creativity and innovation.** By exposing yourself to new ideas and perspectives, you foster creativity and innovation, and find new and innovative solutions to problems. This can also help the company to stay ahead of the curve and stay competitive in a rapidly changing business environment.

- **Increased confidence.** By facing your fears and stepping out of your comfort zone, you build confidence in your abilities and decision making. This helps you to become a more effective leader and to navigate challenges and obstacles with greater ease.

- **Career advancement.** By taking on new challenges and responsibilities, you demonstrate your leadership potential and advance your career. You will also gain recognition and respect of your colleagues, which can lead to further opportunities for growth and development.

But stepping out of your comfort zone is scary, and it's natural to feel fear and resistance. It is important to recognize that fear and resistance are normal reactions to novelty, but also that they can be overcome. Seek support and work to develop a growth mindset.

To succeed in leading a change process, you must embrace change and be willing to take risks. Open up to new ideas and perspectives, and actively seek out opportunities to learn and grow. Be willing to take on new challenges and stay resilient in the face of adversity.

Stepping out of your comfort zone can have a profound impact on your personal journey. By getting used to embracing change and taking risks, you will develop the skills and knowledge that are needed to be an effective leader. With these skills you can foster creativity and innovation and build confidence in your abilities and decision making.

Overcoming fear and resistance. Stepping out of your comfort zone is scary, and it's natural to feel fear and resistance. Fear of failure, fear of the unknown, and fear of change can all hold you back and prevent you from reaching you full potential. Fear and resistance are normal reactions, but they can be overcome.

To overcome fears and resistance you need to develop a growth mindset. This means embracing challenges and seeing them as opportunities for growth, rather than as threats. Here, it may be necessary to seek out support from a mentor who can provide guidance and encouragement as you navigate the challenges and obstacles along the way.

In addition, you can work to develop resilience by cultivating a positive attitude. This is sometimes easier said than done. Focus on your personal strengths and successes. Be open to feedback and constructive criticism. And work to continuously improve skills and knowledge.

Finally, recognize that success often requires taking risks and embracing change. By beginning by taking small steps outside of your comfort zone, you can build confidence and resilience, and gradually expand your comfort zone over time.

Overcoming fear and resistance is an important part of any personal journey. With determination and resilience, you can navigate the challenges and obstacles along the way and achieve success with greater ease and confidence. Throughout your journey, remember that failures are learning opportunities, not an end-state.

Embracing change and taking risks. To become successful, you must learn to embrace change and how to handle risk. Change is a constant in today's rapidly evolving business environment, and you must be prepared to adapt and evolve to succeed. This means constantly being open to learning, new ideas and perspectives, and being willing to take on new challenges and responsibilities.

Work on becoming willing to take risks, even if there is substantial risk of failure. Be proactive in seeking out opportunities for growth and development. Be open to feedback and constructive criticism, and work continuously to improve your skills and knowledge. Seek out new challenges and responsibilities.

Be resilient in the face of adversity. Be willing to persevere even in the face of obstacles and challenges. You need to be determined to succeed.

The impact of stepping out of your comfort zone on your life' **journey**. By learning to embracing change and taking risks, you will develop general skills and knowledge needed to be an effective leader. Together with fostering creativity and innovation, you will build confidence in your abilities and decision making.

Stepping out of your comfort zone is necessary to navigate the challenges and obstacles in life with greater ease and resilience. Take advantage of new opportunities for growth and development. Build relationships and networks that will serve you well in the future.

Your personal growth can also influence others. Stepping out of your comfort zone can help to foster a culture of growth and development within the organization. Share your experiences and lessons learned with others. Inspire others to step outside of their comfort zones and embrace change. This will help to create a supportive environment for all and build a more adaptive and resilient organization.

Stepping out of your comfort zone is an essential part of your life's journey. With determination and resilience, you can navigate the challenges and obstacles along the way and achieve success with greater ease and confidence. By embracing change and taking risks, you can lead the company towards a brighter future and help to create a more adaptive and resilient organization.

Company development

The key elements of an adaptive company culture. An adaptive company culture is the foundation for a successful Darwinian approach to management. It is the driving force behind a company's ability to change, evolve, and thrive in a rapidly changing business environment. Here are some key elements that make up an adaptive company culture.

- **Embracing change**. Companies that embrace change are more likely to survive and succeed in the long run. A culture that encourages change and encourages employees to experiment and try new things is more likely to lead to innovation and growth.

- **Open communication**. Effective communication is essential to the success of an adaptive company culture. Encouraging open and honest dialogue between employees, teams, and leadership is crucial in ensuring that everyone is on the same page and working towards the same goals.

- **Collaboration.** Cooperation is the human superpower. When employees work together, they can share ideas and knowledge, and leverage each other's strengths to achieve greater results.

- **Learning and growth.** In an adaptive company culture, learning and growth are a priority. Employees must be encouraged to continuously improve their personal skills and knowledge, and the company provides resources and opportunities for professional development.

- **Empowerment.** When employees feel empowered, they are more likely to take initiative, be creative, and drive success.

- **Adaptive leadership.** Adaptive leaders lead by example, encourage change, and create an environment that fosters growth and learning.

Strategies for fostering an adaptive company culture. Building an adaptive company culture requires effort and commitment from leadership and employees alike. Here are some strategies for fostering a culture of change and evolution.

- **Lead by example.** Leaders play a critical role in setting the tone for the company culture. By demonstrating a willingness to embrace change and evolve, leaders inspire and encourage their teams to do the same.

- **Encourage experimentation.** Encouraging employees to experiment and try new things that lead to innovation and growth. Companies need to provide resources and support for experimentation to create an environment that rewards risk-taking and encourages learning from failure.

- **Provide opportunities for growth and learning.** Investing in employee development is key to fostering a culture of growth and evolution. Providing training, workshops, and other opportunities for professional development helps employees to continuously improve their skills and knowledge.

- **Foster open communication**. Encouraging open communication is critical to building an adaptive culture. Regular team meetings, one-on-one conversations, and other opportunities for employees to share ideas and feedback can help to ensure that everyone is working towards the same goals.

- **Reward success and resilience**. Rewarding employees for their successes and their ability to navigate challenges and overcome obstacles helps to foster a culture of resilience and perseverance.

- **Encourage collaboration**. Collaboration is key to success in an adaptive culture. Companies foster collaboration by encouraging team-building activities, cross-functional projects, and other opportunities for employees to work together.

The role of leadership in shaping the company culture. Leadership plays a critical role in shaping the company culture and fostering an environment that is open to change and evolution. Here are some ways that leadership can help to build an adaptive culture.

- **Communicate a clear vision**. Leaders should communicate a clear vision for the company and align company culture around this vision. This helps to ensure that everyone is working towards the same goals, and that the company is adapting in a direction that is in line with its goals and values.

- **Model the desired behavior**. Leaders set the tone for the company culture by modeling the behavior and attitudes that they want to see in their employees. For example, if leaders are committed to embracing change and experimentation, they should demonstrate this in their own behavior and decision-making.

- **Foster a sense of belonging**. Creating a sense of belonging and community within the company is key to building a strong company culture. Leaders can foster this sense of belonging by encouraging team-building activities, promoting open communication, and creating opportunities for employees to get to know each other.

- **Encourage collaboration.** We keep getting back to cooperation because it is so important. Leaders encourage collaboration by promoting cross-functional projects and other opportunities for employees to work together. Collaboration helps to foster a sense of shared purpose and promotes the sharing of ideas and knowledge.

- **Celebrate successes.** Leaders help to foster a positive company culture by celebrating the successes of their employees and the company. Recognizing and rewarding employees for their hard work and achievements helps to create a sense of pride and commitment.

- **Encourage continuous improvement.** Leaders encourage continuous improvement by providing opportunities for employee development and by creating an environment that rewards risk-taking and learning from failure.

Leadership has a significant impact on the company culture. By taking an active role in shaping and fostering an adaptive culture, leaders can ensure that their companies are well-equipped to navigate the challenges and opportunities of a rapidly changing business environment.

Embracing a growth mindset and the importance of continuous learning. In a rapidly changing business environment, it is essential for organizations to embrace a growth mindset and a willingness to continuously learn and adapt. This is the first step towards successfully implementing the Darwinian approach to management.

A growth mindset is characterized by an attitude of continuous learning and a belief in one's ability to develop and grow. This mindset is essential in today's business world, where rapid change and innovation are the norm. Organizations must foster a culture of continuous learning and development to stay ahead of the curve.

One way to foster a growth mindset is through encouraging experimentation and taking calculated risks. This allows individuals and teams within the organization to try new things, learn from their mistakes and continue to grow. Encouraging a growth mindset also means recognizing and valuing the potential for growth in all employees and providing opportunities for professional development.

Continuous learning is also essential for organizations in a rapidly changing business environment. This means staying up to date with the latest trends, technologies, and best practices in the industry. It is important for leaders to lead by example and prioritize ongoing learning and development for themselves and their teams.

Developing a culture of experimentation and risk-taking. As we have seen, one of the key principles of the Darwinian approach to management is to embrace change and continuously adapt to new circumstances. This requires a company culture that supports a willingness to take risks and experiment with new ideas and approaches. By developing a culture of experimentation and risk-taking, organizations can cultivate an environment that fosters innovation and creativity.

But how can organizations cultivate this type of culture? The first step is to shift away from a traditional, risk-averse approach to one that is more open to new ideas and approaches. This can be achieved through leadership that supports and encourages experimentation, as well as by establishing a reward system that recognizes and celebrates success.

It is important for leaders to create an environment where employees feel comfortable taking risks and experimenting with new ideas. This can be achieved through regular training and development programs, as well as through the provision of resources and support to employees who are working on new projects or initiatives.

Leaders play a critical role in setting the tone for the organization and creating a culture that supports change and evolution. This may involve providing clear direction and vision, setting high standards for performance, and fostering a positive work environment. Leaders must communicate effectively with all employees and be transparent about the company's goals.

Leaders set the tone for the rest of the organization and demonstrate that it is okay to embrace new ideas and approaches. By creating an environment of openness and trust, leaders can encourage their employees to be more innovative and to take calculated risks.

Another key component of successfully implementing the Darwinian approach is building a team that is open to change and willing to embrace the new approach. Encourage open and honest communication and be transparent about the reasons for change and its potential benefits.

It is also important to recognize and reward those who are willing to take risks and embrace new ideas. This helps to create a positive reinforcement culture that encourages experimentation and risk-taking in others. Additionally, providing training and support to help employees adapt to the new approach will help build confidence and reduce resistance to change.

Foster a sense of collaboration and teamwork within the organization. Encourage cross-functional collaboration, and work to break down interdepartmental silos to create a more unified and cohesive team. Company success is achieved together.

5 EMBRACING EXPERIMENTATION
AND FAILURE

Experimentation is essential for driving innovation and progress in the business world. By constantly trying new ideas and approaches, companies can identify what works and what doesn't, and make informed decisions that lead to success. Experimentation can take many forms, from small tests to major initiatives.

One of the benefits of small-scale experimentation is that it helps to mitigate risk. By testing new ideas in a controlled environment, companies can gather data and insights that can help them make more informed decisions. This can help avoid costly mistakes and increase the likelihood of success. But all experimentation provides an opportunity to learn and grow. By trying new things and learning from failures, companies can improve and adapt over time.

Another benefit of experimentation is that it can lead to breakthrough innovations. By constantly pushing the boundaries of what is possible and testing new ideas, companies can create new products and services that differentiate them from their competitors. This leads to significant competitive advantages and helps companies stay ahead of the curve.

Experimentation is the crucial tool for companies that are looking to succeed in a rapidly changing business environment. By embracing experimentation and encouraging risk-taking, companies can innovate, learn from their failures, and increase their chances of success.

The benefits of allowing failure. One of the key benefits of embracing experimentation is that it allows for failure. While embracing failure may seem counterintuitive, the truth is that failure can be incredibly valuable. By allowing for the possibility of failure, companies can create a culture where risk-taking and innovation are encouraged. In fact, there is no risk-taking without failure. Embracing failure leads to a greater willingness to try new things, which in turn can lead to greater innovation and success.

Allowing for failure also helps to mitigate risk. When companies are afraid of failure, they are less likely to take risks and try new things. This can stifle innovation and lead to missed opportunities. By embracing failure, companies create a culture where risk-taking is encouraged and where it is seen as a necessary part of the learning and growth process.

Furthermore, failures are valuable learning experiences. By studying what went wrong and what can be done better in the future, companies can improve and become more efficient. This learning process leads to a better understanding of the company's strengths and weaknesses, which in turn helps to inform future decisions.

Allowing for failure is a central aspect of the Darwinian approach to management. By embracing failure and learning from it, companies foster a culture of risk-taking and innovation, mitigate risk, and become better equipped to succeed in a rapidly changing business environment.

However, despite the benefits of embracing failure, many companies and individuals are still afraid of it. This is understandable, but fear can be a major obstacle to embracing a Darwinian approach to management and creating a culture of change and evolution. Herein lies the greatest challenge for a company embracing an adaptive approach.

To overcome this fear, companies must understand the difference between a fixed mindset and a growth mindset. **A fixed mindset** is the belief that our abilities and talents are set in stone and cannot be changed. This type of mindset is often associated with the fear of failure, as individuals with a fixed mindset may be afraid of trying new things and failing, as it may reveal a lack of talent or ability.

A growth mindset, on the other hand, is the belief that our abilities and talents can be developed and improved through hard work and perseverance. This type of mindset is essential for embracing a Darwinian approach to management, as it encourages individuals to take risks and embrace experimentation. What you want for your company is to encourage a growth mindset.

To foster a growth mindset, companies must create an environment that is supportive and encouraging of risk-taking and experimentation. This includes providing opportunities for growth and recognizing and rewarding risk-taking and innovation. Companies can also provide resources for employees to help them overcome their fear of failure and develop a growth mindset.

Additionally, companies encourage a growth mindset by embracing a culture of learning and continuous improvement. This includes encouraging employees to learn from their failures and to use those lessons to inform future decisions. Continuously provide employees with learning opportunities and encourage their participation in them.

There is no way around it. Overcoming the fear of failure and embracing a growth mindset is essential for creating a culture of change. By fostering a supportive environment, providing opportunities for growth and development, and encouraging a culture of learning and continuous improvement, companies encourage individuals to take risks and embrace experimentation. This what ultimately will lead the company to success.

The importance of experimentation in the pursuit of success.
Experimentation is the cornerstone of progress and innovation in the business world. It is the act of testing new ideas, methods, and processes to determine their effectiveness and suitability. In an ever-changing business environment, experimentation is crucial to stay ahead of the curve and stay competitive.

Embracing experimentation means being open to new ideas and being willing to try new things. For many organizations, experimentation is seen as a cost, a risk, and a potential source of failure.

However, experimentation allows organizations to test new ideas and processes in a controlled environment, and to make informed decisions based on the results. By embracing experimentation, organizations can quickly determine what works and what doesn't, and make the necessary changes to stay ahead of the curve.

To be successful in today's rapidly changing business environment, organizations must embrace experimentation as a key part of their operations. This requires a shift in mindset, from one of fear and caution, to one of resilience and determination. It requires leaders to foster a culture of experimentation and risk-taking, and to encourage their teams to embrace new ideas and challenge the status quo.

By being open to new ideas, embracing failure, and continuously testing and refining their operations, organizations can stay ahead of the curve and achieve success in a rapidly changing business environment.

The benefits of allowing failure. Not all experiments will be successful. The ability to embrace failure is a key component of a growth mindset and fostering it can provide many benefits for an organization.

First, allowing failure helps to promote the culture of experimentation and innovation. When employees know that it is acceptable to try new things and that failure is not only expected, but also accepted, they will be more likely to take risks and suggest new ideas. This leads to new products, services, and processes that help the company to stay ahead of the curve and grow.

Second, failure can be a valuable learning experience. When an experiment doesn't work, it can provide valuable insights into what did and didn't work. This information can then be used to improve future experiments, making them more likely to be successful.

Finally, embracing failure can help to build resilience. By recognizing that failure is a normal part of the experimentation process, organizations learn to bounce back from setbacks and continue moving forward. This resilience is essential in a rapidly changing business environment, where organizations must be able to adapt and overcome obstacles to thrive.

Embracing experimentation and allowing failure is a critical component of an adaptive organization. By creating a culture that supports risk-taking and learning from failure, organizations can encourage innovation, build resilience, and ultimately achieve their goals.

Overcoming the fear of failure and embracing a growth mindset.
Despite the proven importance of experimentation and failure, many
organizations struggle to embrace them. Fear of failure is a powerful
deterrent, causing people to cling to the status quo instead of taking risks
and trying new things. People with a growth mindset are more open to
experimentation and less afraid of failure because they see it as an
opportunity for growth and learning. Here are some tools to encourage a
growth mindset within an organization.

- **Lead by example.** Encourage leaders and managers to embrace
  experimentation and failure. When they model this behavior, it
  becomes easier for others to follow suit.

- **Celebrate failure.** Highlight examples of experimentation and
  failure that led to learning and growth. Celebrating this process
  helps to break down the stigma around failure and encourages
  others to embrace it. Whether it's through financial incentives or
  recognition programs, recognizing and rewarding employees for
  their innovative ideas and initiatives helps build a culture of
  creativity and risk-taking.

- **Reframe failure.** Instead of viewing failure as a negative outcome,
  reframe it as an essential part of the learning process. This mindset
  shift helps to reduce the fear of failure and encourages
  experimentation. Do not forget the importance of incentives – they
  are just as important when celebrating success as when recognizing
  learning through failure.

- **Reward risk-taking.** Encourage a culture that supports and
  encourages risk-taking. Provide resources and support for
  experimentation and learning, and reward people for taking risks
  and trying new things.

- **Provide employees with a sense of autonomy and trust.**
  Allowing employees to work on projects and initiatives without
  close supervision, and trusting them to make decisions, leads to an
  environment of innovation and creativity. Innovation can't be
  ordered.

- **Provide resources**. Give your team the resources they need to experiment and be creative. This could mean providing budget for R&D, access to technology, or even time to explore new ideas.

The importance of continuous learning and staying ahead of the curve. In today's rapidly changing business environment, staying ahead of the curve is essential for success. One of the keys to staying ahead is continuous learning and innovation. By embracing a culture that supports innovation and experimentation, organizations foster creativity and risk-taking, and can remain at the forefront of their industry.

Continuous learning is a critical component of innovation. Employees who are encouraged to seek out new information and knowledge are more likely to come up with creative solutions to challenges and problems. This can be achieved by providing employees with opportunities to attend workshops, conferences, and other training programs, as well as by encouraging them to read books and articles on topics related to their field.

To stay ahead of the curve, organizations must also foster a culture that supports risk-taking and experimentation. This means creating a safe and supportive environment where employees feel comfortable taking risks and trying new things. This can be achieved through open communication and collaboration, as well as by recognizing and rewarding innovative ideas and solutions.

6 THE CROSSROADS OF DECISION: LEADING WITH RESILIENCE

Now you may find yourself at a crossroads, faced with a critical decision that will impact the future of the company – to go Darwinian or not? Before making any moves, try to envision the consequences of your choices. Examine the potential outcomes of different decisions and consider the impact they will have on the company and its stakeholders. Consider the following.

- What are the short-term and long-term consequences of each option? Can you keep doing the same thing or do you need to adapt to survive and thrive?

- How will the decision affect the company's financial stability? There may be initial costs to encouraging experimentation, stressing continuous learning and – not the least – embracing failure.

- Will the decision impact the company's reputation and brand image? Perhaps you are known for a very specific product or service. How will new thinking be received?

- What impact will the decision have on employees, customers, and other stakeholders? Everyone is not comfortable with experiments and failure. Should you listen to them, or should they listen to you?

By taking the time to understand the consequences of your choices, you can make decisions that aligns with the company's values and goals and helps to ensure its success in the future.

Gather information. It is crucial to gather information to inform your decision. This involves researching the options, gathering data, and seeking the advice and input of experts and trusted advisors. To gather the information you need, these are some methods.

- Research the options. Conduct a thorough investigation of each option, including market trends, industry insights, and expert opinions. This will help you to fully understand the potential outcomes and benefits of each choice.

- Seek advice from experts. Consult with industry experts and trusted advisors who have experience in the area you are facing. They can provide valuable insights and guidance to help inform your decision.

- Gather data. Collect data and information that will help you to make an informed decision. This may include financial projections, market research, and customer feedback.

By gathering information from a variety of sources, you can ensure that you have all the information you need to make a confident and well-informed decision.

Weighing the pros and cons. With a clearer understanding of the potential consequences of each option and the information you have gathered, it's time to weigh the pros and cons of each choice. This involves identifying the strengths and weaknesses of each option and evaluating the risks and benefits of each decision.

- Identify strengths and weaknesses. Consider advantages and disadvantages of each option. What are the benefits and drawbacks of each choice, and how do they align with the company's values and goals?

- Evaluate risks and benefits. Assess risks and benefits associated with each decision. What is the potential impact of each choice, and how will it affect the company and its stakeholders?

By thoroughly weighing the pros and cons of each option, you can make a decision that is in the best interest of the company and its future success.

Making the decision. With a clearer understanding of the consequences of each option, the information you have gathered, and the pros and cons weighed, it's time to make the decision. This requires careful consideration of the company's values, goals, and mission, as well as the perspectives and opinions of others.

- Consider company values, goals, and mission. Make sure that the decision aligns with the company's values and goals and supports its mission.

- Consider perspectives and opinions of others. Listen to the opinions and perspectives of employees, customers, and other stakeholders. How will the decision impact them, and what are their concerns and needs?

- Consider the potential for future growth and success. Look to the future and consider the potential for growth and success for the company. What is the long-term impact of the decision, and how will it help the company to succeed in the future?

By taking all these factors into consideration, you can make a decision that is in the best interest of the company, its stakeholders, and its future success.

Implementing the decision. Having made the decision, it's time to implement it. This requires a plan for implementation, effective communication with all stakeholders, and the management of any challenges or obstacles that may arise during the process.

- Develop a plan for implementation. Create a proposal for how to implement the decision, including a timeline, responsibilities, and any necessary resources.

- Communicate the decision to all stakeholders. Ensure that all stakeholders are informed of the decision and understand the reasons behind it.

- Manage any challenges or obstacles. Be prepared to manage any challenges or obstacles that may arise during the implementation process. This may involve addressing concerns, finding solutions to problems, and adjusting as necessary.

By following a clear and well-planned implementation process, you can ensure that the decision is executed effectively, and that the company is on the path to success.

The role of leadership in navigating change and adversity. Leadership is critical in shaping and guiding an organization, especially during times of change and adversity. This is about you. A resilient leader must possess a combination of determination, vision, and emotional intelligence to successfully steer the company through uncertain waters. A leader must be able to inspire and motivate their team, communicate effectively, and make tough decisions when necessary.

Change is inevitable in today's rapidly evolving business landscape, and leaders must be prepared to navigate these challenges and help their teams navigate them as well. Resilience is key to success, and leaders must model this behavior for their teams. They must lead by example and show that it is possible to persevere through adversity and come out stronger on the other side.

Leadership also plays a crucial role in shaping the company culture, as leaders set the tone and expectations for the rest of the organization. In the context of a Darwinian approach to management, leaders must be open-minded, embrace experimentation and failure, and encourage their teams to do the same. They must foster a culture of continuous improvement and be willing to take calculated risks to drive the company forward.

The role of leadership in navigating change and adversity is critical to the success of an adaptive organization. Leaders must possess resilience, determination, emotional intelligence, and lead by example to inspire and motivate their teams. By doing so, they will help to shape a company culture that is equipped to thrive in a rapidly changing business environment.

Characteristics of resilient leaders. Resilient leaders can navigate challenges and adversity in a calm and confident manner, and they need to foster key characteristics that allow them to do so.

- **Emotional intelligence**. Resilient leaders need a high level of emotional intelligence, which allows them to understand and manage their own emotions as well as the emotions of those around them. This helps them to maintain a level of stability and focus during times of stress and uncertainty.

- **Adaptability**. Resilient leaders need to adapt to new situations and challenges quickly, and not be afraid to try new things. They should be open to change and able to adjust their strategies as necessary to achieve their goals.

- **Determination**. Resilient leaders should be determined to succeed, and they never give up, even in the face of obstacles and setbacks. They need a strong sense of purpose and are committed to their goals.

- **Communication skills**. Resilient leaders should communicate effectively, both with their teams and with stakeholders. They should articulate their vision and goals clearly and listen to the perspectives and ideas of others.

- **Self-awareness**. Resilient leaders need a strong sense of self-awareness and understand their own strengths and weaknesses. This allows them to seek help and support when necessary and to continuously improve their leadership skills.

- **Optimism**. Resilient leaders need to be optimistic, especially in the face of challenges. They should communicate a belief in their ability to overcome adversity and maintain a positive outlook. This helps the team to maintain a level of energy and motivation even during difficult times.

- **Mental toughness**. Resilient leaders need to foster a strong and resilient mindset to be able to maintain a positive outlook even in the face of setbacks and challenges. They need to learn how to bounce back quickly from setbacks and keep their focus on the bigger picture.

- **Vision and determination**. Resilient leaders should maintain a clear vision for their company and be determined to see it through, no matter what obstacles they may face. This inspires their teams to work towards a common goal and keep everyone focused and motivated.

Leadership plays a crucial role in guiding a company through change and adversity, and the characteristics of resilient leaders can greatly impact the success of navigating these challenges. Resilient leaders need to foster certain qualities that enable them to remain focused and composed in difficult times and inspire their teams to do the same. By maintaining and fostering these characteristics, resilient leaders will be able to guide their companies through change and adversity, and ultimately lead them to success.

Strategies for Developing Resilience in Leaders and Employees. Resilience is a critical quality for anyone in a leadership role, especially in today's rapidly changing business environment. Resilient leaders can navigate adversity, bounce back from setbacks, and continue to lead their organizations forward. Here are some simple strategies for developing resilience in both leaders and employees.

- **Exercise**. Regular exercise has numerous benefits for physical and mental health, including increased resilience. Exercise helps individuals develop the physical and mental toughness they need to face challenges and bounce back from setbacks.

- **Mindfulness**. Mindfulness practices, such as meditation and deep breathing, have been shown to increase resilience. By taking time to focus on the present moment, leaders and employees can cultivate a greater sense of control over their thoughts and emotions, reducing stress and increasing their ability to handle difficult situations.

- **Develop a growth mindset**. A growth mindset, in which individuals view setbacks as opportunities for growth and learning, helps to foster resilience. By focusing on the process of growth rather than just the outcome, individuals develop a more positive outlook and become better equipped to handle adversity.

- **Maintain a support system**. Having a supportive network of friends, family, and colleagues is critical for building resilience. Having people to lean on for emotional support and encouragement can help individuals bounce back from setbacks and maintain determination to succeed.

- **Focus on self-care**. Taking care of oneself is essential for maintaining resilience. Leaders and employees should prioritize activities that bring them joy, relaxation, and a sense of balance, such as hobbies, spending time with loved ones, or simply taking a break from work.

- **Seek professional help**. If an individual is struggling with resilience, it may be helpful to seek the support of a mental health professional. A therapist can provide support, guidance, and tools to help individuals overcome challenges and build resilience.

By incorporating these strategies into their daily routine, leaders and employees can develop the resilience they need to navigate adversity and lead their organizations to success. With a focus on personal growth, self-care, and support, individuals can become more resilient, better equipped to handle challenges, and ultimately more successful in their roles.

The role of leadership in navigating change and adversity.
Leadership is an essential ingredient in navigating change and adversity within an organization. As the company faces the challenges of a rapidly changing business environment, leaders must be able to inspire and guide their team through uncertainty and adversity. In a Darwinian approach to management, leaders must be resilient, adaptive, and forward-thinking, leading their team to success in the face of adversity.

Leadership in this context requires a deep understanding of the principles of natural selection and the importance of adaptation. Leaders must be able to recognize and respond to the challenges of change, navigating the organization through the ups and downs of the journey. This requires a focus on continuous learning, experimentation, and risk-taking, while also being able to balance short-term and long-term goals.

Leaders must also be able to inspire and motivate their team, building a culture of resilience and collaboration. This requires fostering a positive attitude towards change and adversity and embracing a growth mindset that views failures as opportunities for growth and learning. With the right mindset and approach, leaders can steer their organization to success in the face of change and adversity.

7 PROOF OF CONCEPT:
EVALUATING AND IMPROVING PERFORMANCE

In the world of business, it is critical to measure progress and make data-driven decisions to continuously improve and reach your goals. Tracking progress allows a company to identify areas where they excel, as well as areas where they may need to make changes to improve. This information can then be used to make informed decisions that drive growth and success.

Only by asking the right questions will you know how the change process is going. But what questions that are right will differ between companies.

Key tools to track progress are performance metrics. These metrics help a company evaluate its performance in areas such as sales, customer satisfaction, employee engagement, and efficiency. Regularly monitoring these metrics provides a clear picture of how the company is performing and allows for data-driven decision making.

Another important aspect of tracking progress is regularly conducting performance reviews. These reviews provide a forum for employees and managers to discuss progress, identify areas for improvement, and set goals for future development. This also includes regular check-ins to ensure that employees are on track to meet their goals and making progress in the right direction.

Using data and tracking progress is not only important for the success of the company, but also for the growth and development of employees.

Regular performance evaluations provide employees with feedback on their strengths and areas for improvement, allowing them to take ownership of their own development.

Strategies for evaluating and improving performance. Evaluating and improving performance is a crucial aspect of building successful and adaptive organizations. To continuously improve, it is important to have a clear understanding of your current performance and identify areas for growth. Here are some strategies for evaluating and improving performance.

- **Set clear goals and objectives**. Start by setting clear and measurable goals for the company and its employees. This will help everyone understand what is expected and give them something specific to work towards.

- **Carry out regular performance evaluations**. Regular performance evaluations are a key tool for evaluating and improving performance. They provide a forum for managers and employees to discuss progress, identify areas for improvement, and set goals for future development.

- **Use performance metrics**. Performance metrics can provide valuable insights into the performance of the company and its employees. Regularly monitoring these metrics can help identify areas for improvement and inform data-driven decision making.

- **Encourage employee feedback**. Employee feedback is a valuable tool for improving performance. Encourage employees to share their thoughts and opinions on how they feel the company can improve. This can help identify areas for improvement and drive employee engagement.

- **Continuously learn and adapt**. Encourage employees to continuously develop their skills and embrace new ideas and methods. This will help the company stay ahead of the curve and stay competitive in a rapidly changing business environment.

By using these strategies, a company can continuously evaluate and improve its performance, leading to increased success and a more adaptive organization. Remember, evaluating and improving performance is a continuous process, not a one-time event, so it is important to consistently evaluate and make changes as needed.

The role of continuous improvement in building an adaptive organization. In a rapidly changing business environment, it is crucial for organizations to be able to adapt and evolve to stay ahead of the competition. One of the key elements of an adaptive organization is a culture of continuous improvement, where data and performance metrics are used to inform decisions and drive progress. By regularly evaluating and improving performance, organizations can stay nimble and responsive to changing market conditions, customer needs, and emerging opportunities.

To effectively evaluate and improve performance, it is important to have a system in place for tracking progress and collecting data. As outlined previously, this can involve regularly monitoring key performance indicators such as sales figures, customer satisfaction, employee engagement, and process efficiency. By tracking these metrics, organizations can gain a clear picture of how they are performing and identify areas that need improvement.

Also, as already mentioned, feedback from employees and customers can provide valuable insights into areas where the organization is performing well and areas that need improvement. It can also help leaders identify trends and patterns that may not be immediately apparent from the data.

Once the data has been collected, use it to make informed decisions. Leaders should take the time to analyze the data and identify areas where changes can be made to improve performance. This involves making changes to processes, policies, and systems, as well as investing in training and development programs to improve skills and knowledge.

Organizations promote continuous improvement by implementing continuous improvement processes. A structured approach to improvement helps organizations to identify and prioritize opportunities for improvement, and to implement changes quickly and efficiently. Such processes should be viewed as a never-ending journey, with regular evaluations and improvements made to ensure that the organization remains adaptive and responsive to changing conditions.

Continuous improvement is the key element of an adaptive organization and is essential for organizations to stay competitive in a rapidly changing business environment. By regularly tracking performance, encouraging experimentation and innovation, and implementing a structured approach to improvement, organizations promote a culture of continuous improvement that drives growth and success.

Building a Business Case. To convince others of the value of the Darwinian approach, it's important to build a compelling business case that clearly outlines the problem, solution, and benefits. A well-constructed business case should be easy to understand, visually appealing, and persuasive.

The first step in building a business case is to identify key stakeholders, including decision makers and influencers, and understand their motivations and concerns. This will help you tailor your argument to address their specific needs and objections.

Next, you need to define the problem and outline the solution. This involves identifying the challenges faced by the organization and how the Darwinian approach addresses those challenges. It's important to be specific and concrete, using data and case studies to illustrate the benefits of the approach.

Finally, you need to present the business case in a clear and compelling way. This may involve using visuals, such as charts and graphs, to illustrate the benefits of the Darwinian approach, as well as telling stories that illustrate its impact in real-world situations.

- **Identify key stakeholders**. This includes decision makers and influencers who will play a role in the adoption of the Darwinian approach. Understanding their motivations and concerns will help you tailor your argument to address their specific needs and objections.

- **Define the problem**. This involves identifying the challenges faced by the organization and the impact they have on key metrics such as productivity, innovation, and employee engagement.

- **Outline the solution**. This involves describing the Darwinian approach and how it addresses the challenges identified. It's important to be specific and concrete, using data and case studies to illustrate the benefits of the approach.

- **Present the business case**. This involves presenting the information gathered in the precious steps in a clear and compelling way. Use visuals, such as charts and graphs, to illustrate the benefits of the Darwinian approach, and tell stories that illustrate its impact in real-world situations.

- **Address objections**. Anticipate and address objections to the Darwinian approach, such as concerns about change, risk, and culture. Be prepared to provide data and case studies that demonstrate the benefits of the approach and how it has been successfully implemented in other organizations.

By following these steps, you will have the tools you need to build a persuasive business case that convinces others of the value of the Darwinian approach.

Darwinian success stories

Amazon is a prime example of a company that has embraced the Darwinian approach to management. The company is known for its data-driven decision making, rapid iteration, and willingness to experiment and fail fast. These principles are at the heart of the Darwinian approach and have helped Amazon become one of the most innovative and successful companies in the world.

Amazon has used the Darwinian approach to management to become one of the most innovative and successful companies in the world. The key principles of the Darwinian approach, such as data-driven decision making, rapid iteration, and a willingness to experiment and fail fast, are at the core of Amaon's business strategy.

For example, Amazon uses data to make informed decisions about everything from product development to pricing. The company is constantly experimenting with new business models and technologies and is not afraid to fail. This allows Amazon to quickly respond to changes in the market and stay ahead of the competition.

Another key aspect of Amazon's success is its focus on the customer. The company is constantly gathering data on customer preferences and behaviors and using that information to inform its product development and marketing strategies. This customer-centric approach has helped Amazon build a loyal customer base and establish itself as a leader in the e-commerce space.

Overall, Amazon's embrace of the Darwinian approach to management has been a key factor in its success. The company's focus on data, experimentation, and rapid iteration has allowed it to quickly respond to changes in the market and stay ahead of the competition.

Netflix is another company that has embraced the Darwinian approach to management. The company's focus on data and its willingness to experiment has allowed it to disrupt the traditional entertainment industry and become a leader in the streaming space.

For example, Netflix uses data to inform its content strategy, making decisions about what shows to produce, how to market them, and when to release them. The company is constantly experimenting with new business models and technologies and is not afraid to fail. This allows Netflix to quickly respond to changes in the market and stay ahead of the competition.

Another key aspect of Netflix's success is its focus on the customer. The company is constantly gathering data on customer preferences and behaviors and using that information to inform its content strategy. This customer-centric approach has helped Netflix build a loyal customer base and establish itself as a leader in the streaming video industry.

Overall, Netflix's embrace of the Darwinian approach to management has been a key factor in its success. The company's focus on data, experimentation, and rapid iteration has allowed it to quickly respond to changes in the market and stay ahead of the competition. By continuously adapting to the changing needs of its customers and the market, Netflix has become one of the most successful and innovative companies in the world.

Google is a company that is synonymous with innovation and agility. The company's focus on data and its willingness to experiment have allowed it to stay at the forefront of technology and maintain its position as one of the most valuable companies in the world.

Google has used the Darwinian approach to management to become one of the most innovative and successful companies in the world. The key principles of the Darwinian approach, such as data-driven decision making, rapid iteration, and a willingness to experiment and fail fast, are at the core of Google's business strategy.

For example, Google uses data to inform its product development, making decisions about what features to add, how to improve existing products, and when to launch new products. The company is constantly experimenting with new technologies and business models. It has separate experimental departments that are allowed to experiment and fail. This allows Google to quickly respond to changes in the market and stay ahead of the competition.

Google is constantly gathering data on user preferences and behaviors. It then uses that information to inform its product development. This user-centric approach has helped Google build a loyal user base and establish itself as a leader in the technology industry.

Overall, Google's embrace of the Darwinian approach to management has been a key factor in its success. By continuously adapting to the changing needs of its users and the market, Google has become one of the most successful and innovative companies in the world.

Tesla is a company that has embraced the Darwinian approach to management to disrupt the traditional automotive industry. This has allowed it to quickly bring new and innovative products to market and establish itself as a leader in the electric vehicle space.

Tesla uses data to inform its product development, making decisions about what features to add, how to improve existing products, and when to launch new products. The company is constantly experimenting with new technologies and business models and is not afraid to fail. This allows Tesla to quickly respond to changes in the market and stay ahead of the competition.

Another key aspect of Tesla's success is its focus on sustainability. The company is constantly gathering data on the environmental impact of its products and using that information to inform its product development. This sustainability-focused approach has helped Tesla build a loyal customer base and establish itself as a leader in the electric vehicle space. Overall, Tesla's embrace of the Darwinian approach to management has been a key factor in its success.

Spotify is a music streaming service that has used the Darwinian approach to management to its benefit to become one of the most popular and successful services of its kind. The company's focus on data and its willingness to experiment have allowed it to quickly respond to changes in the market and stay ahead of the competition.

Spotify uses data to inform its product development, making decisions about what features to add, how to improve existing products, and when to launch new products. The company is constantly experimenting with new business models and technologies. This allows Spotify to quickly respond to changes in the market and stay ahead of the competition.

Another key aspect of Spotify's success is its focus on the user. The company is constantly gathering data on user preferences and behaviors and uses that information to inform its product development. This user-centric approach has helped Spotify build a loyal user base and establish itself as a leader in the music streaming space. By continuously adapting to the changing needs of its users and the market, Spotify has become one of the most successful and innovative companies in the world.

Darwinian failure stories

Kodak was once a dominant player in the photography industry but failed to adapt to the digital age. The company was slow to embrace digital technology and was not willing to experiment with new business models, which ultimately led to its downfall.

Kodak is a prime example of a company that failed to embrace the Darwinian approach to management and therefore failed. The company was once a dominant player in the photography industry but was unwilling to adapt to the digital age.

Kodak did not experiment with new business models or embrace new technologies, such as digital photography. The company was also not willing to embrace data-driven decision making and was slow to respond to changes in the market. This ultimately led to its downfall as it was unable to keep pace with the rapid changes in the photography industry.

Additionally, Kodak was not focused on the customer, and was not willing to gather data on customer preferences and behaviors. This lack of customer focus ultimately hurt the company as it was unable to respond to changes in customer needs and preferences.

Overall, Kodak's failure to embrace the Darwinian approach to management was a key factor in its downfall. The company's unwillingness to experiment with new business models, embrace new technologies, and focus on the customer ultimately led to its decline and eventual failure.

Blockbuster was a video rental chain that failed to adapt to the rise of digital media and the advent of online streaming. The company was slow to embrace new technologies and was not willing to experiment with new business models, which ultimately led to its downfall.

Blockbuster was not willing to experiment with new business models or embrace new technologies, such as online streaming. The company was also not willing to embrace data-driven decision making and was slow to respond to changes in the market. Additionally, Blockbuster was not focused on the customer, and was not willing to gather data on customer preferences and behaviors. This lack of customer focus ultimately hurt the company as it was unable to respond to changes in customer needs and preferences. Blockbuster's failure to embrace the Darwinian approach to management was a key factor in its downfall.

Sears was once a dominant player in the retail industry but failed to adapt to the rise of e-commerce. The company was slow to embrace online shopping and was not willing to experiment with new business models. The company was once a dominant player in the retail industry but was slow to adapt to the rise of e-commerce. Sears' failure to embrace the Darwinian approach to management was a key factor in its downfall.

Blackberry was once a leader in the smartphone market but failed to adapt to the rise of touch-screen devices. The company was slow to embrace new technologies and was not willing to experiment with new business models, which ultimately led to its downfall. Blackberry didn't experiment with new business models or embrace new technologies, such as touch-screen devices.

Additionally, Blackberry was not focused on the customer, and was not willing to gather data on customer preferences and behaviors. This lack of customer focus ultimately hurt the company as it was unable to respond to changes in customer needs and preferences.

Borders was a large book retailer that failed to adapt to the rise of e-commerce and digital books. The company was slow to embrace online shopping and was not willing to experiment with new business models, which ultimately led to its downfall. Borders is also a prime example of a company that failed to embrace the Darwinian approach to management and therefore failed.

The list goes on. You want to be on the list of successful companies.

8 GETTING IT DONE

Now that you know a bit more about Darwinian management, what is stopping you in creating an adaptive work environment? Take a moment to reflect on what stands in your way. Whether it's resistance to change, lack of resources, or simply a lack of understanding, identifying the obstacles is key to developing a plan to overcome them.

As we discussed in Chapter 2, one of the biggest obstacles facing organizations is resistance to change. This can come from yourself, employees, stakeholders, or the organization. It is important to understand the reasons behind this resistance, whether it's fear of the unknown or a belief that the old ways are better. By understanding these motivations, you can tailor your approach to overcome this resistance and move the organization forward.

Another obstacle organizations may face is a lack of resources, whether it's time, money, or manpower. This can be especially challenging in a rapidly changing business environment where success requires quick action and agility. By identifying the resources you have at your disposal and finding creative ways to maximize their impact, you can work to overcome this obstacle.

Finally, a lack of understanding can be a major obstacle. This can be due to a lack of education, a lack of communication, or simply a lack of exposure to new ideas. By actively seeking out information, training, and resources, you can overcome this obstacle and continue to grow and adapt.

So, take a step back and assess your organization's current situation. What obstacles are standing in your way? Go back to Chapter 2, if necessary. By identifying challenges, you can develop a plan of action to overcome them and achieve success.

Developing a Plan of Action. Once you have identified the obstacles standing in your way, the next step is to develop a plan of action to overcome them. This involves creating a roadmap that outlines the steps you need to take to achieve your goals.

- **Set clear and achievable goals**. What do you want to achieve, and how will you measure success? This will give you a clear direction and a way to track progress.

- **Gather a team of allies who will support you in overcoming the obstacles**. This can be co-workers, employees, stakeholders, or other experts in your field. By working together, you can leverage each other's strengths and resources to achieve your goals.

Once you have your team and your goals in place, it's time to start developing the plan of action. Break down obstacles into smaller, manageable steps, and assign responsibilities to different members of the team. It's important to be flexible and adjust the plan as needed, as the business environment is constantly changing.

It is also important to prioritize and allocate resources effectively. This involves making tough decisions about where to focus your efforts and what to invest in. But by taking a strategic approach, you can maximize the impact of your efforts.

With clear goals, a supportive team, and a flexible plan, you are well on your way to overcoming the challenges and achieving success.

Implementing Your Plan. When you have a plan of action, it's time to put it into motion. This involves implementing the steps outlined in the plan and overcoming any resistance that may arise along the way.

As already discussed, one of the biggest challenges in implementing a plan is overcoming resistance to change. It is important to be proactive in addressing this resistance and to understand the motivations behind it. As this is so important, go back to Chapter 2 and read it again if necessary. By communicating clearly, involving employees in the process, and demonstrating the benefits of change, you can overcome this resistance and move the organization forward.

It is essential that most co-workers are on the same page and working towards the same goals. This may involve regular check-ins and progress updates, as well as clear lines of communication and a shared understanding of responsibilities. By keeping everyone informed and involved, you can ensure that everyone is working together towards a common goal.

It's also important to be flexible and adjust the plan as needed. Work and business environments are constantly changing, and what worked yesterday may not work today. By being agile and open to new ideas, you can continuously improve and overcome any obstacles that may arise. Be Darwinian and adaptable also when implementing your plan of action. Stay focused, stay determined, stay resilient, and you will achieve success.

Measuring Success and Adjusting. As you implement your plan, regularly measure your progress and adjust as needed. As outlined in the previous chapter, measure success by tracking your progress against the goals you set in your plan of action. This will give you a clear understanding of what works and what needs to be improved. It's important to be honest and objective in your assessments. Do not shy away from making changes when necessary. Remember to be adaptable.

Gather feedback from employees, stakeholders, and customers. This can give you valuable insights into how your efforts are being perceived and what changes may be necessary to improve. By actively seeking out and responding to feedback, you can continuously improve and adapt to the changing business environment.

Do not forget to stay up to date on industry trends and best practices. By staying informed and continuously learning, you can stay ahead of the curve and make any necessary adjustments to your approach.

Celebrate Success and Improve Continuously. As you overcome challenges, it's important to take moments to celebrate your accomplishments. Recognition and appreciation of hard work and effort put in by everyone involved can help boost morale and encourage continued progress.

Never forget, however, that success in a rapidly changing business environment is a journey, not a destination. In a changing environment you need to keep running just to stay in the same place. Adaptation is a process and not a goal. Challenges and obstacles will continue to arise, and it's important to stay focused and continue to adapt and improve.

Take time to celebrate successes and acknowledge the hard work of everyone involved when it happens. But never rest on your laurels. Keep learning, keep growing, and keep adapting to the changing business environment. By continuously improving, you can ensure that your organization stays ahead of the curve and continues to achieve success. We will look more closely at productive methods to celebrate in Chapter 10.

Common obstacles that may arise during the transition to a Darwinian approach. As an organization transitions to a Darwinian approach to management, it's important to be aware of and prepared for common obstacles that may arise. As we have seen, these can include:

- **Resistance to change**. Employees may be hesitant to embrace new ideas and processes, particularly if they are comfortable with the current way of doing things.
- **Lack of buy-in from stakeholders**. Some stakeholders may be skeptical of the benefits of a Darwinian approach or may have conflicting goals and priorities.
- **Limited resources**. Implementing change can require significant time and resources, which may not be available.
- **Inadequate infrastructure**. The organization may need to invest in new technologies, tools, and processes to support a Darwinian approach.

- **Challenges in data collection and analysis**. The Darwinian approach requires accurate and meaningful data to inform decision-making.
- **Misalignment of objectives**. It's important to ensure that all stakeholders are aligned on the goals of the organization and the benefits of a Darwinian approach.

Strategies for overcoming obstacles and navigating change. To overcome common obstacles that may arise during the transition to a Darwinian approach, organizations can implement the following strategies.

- **Communicate effectively**. Communicating the goals, benefits, and process of the transition to all stakeholders is key to overcoming resistance and building buy-in.
- **Foster a culture of change**. Encourage a growth mindset, celebrate both successes and failures as opportunities for learning, and create an environment that supports experimentation and risk-taking.
- **Allocate resources appropriately**. Ensure that the necessary time, money, and resources are available to support the transition and implement change effectively.
- **Invest in technology and infrastructure**. Implementing new technologies, tools, and processes can help organizations better collect, analyze, and use data to inform decision-making.
- **Align objectives**. Ensure that all stakeholders are aligned on the goals of the organization and the benefits of a Darwinian approach, and involve stakeholders in the decision-making process to build commitment and buy-in.
- **Embrace continuous improvement**. Continuously monitor progress, collect and analyze data, and make improvements based on that data. Celebrate small wins and acknowledge areas for improvement. Continuously evolve the organization to meet changing needs.

The Importance of Perseverance and Determination in the Face of Adversity. The journey to build an adaptive organization is not without its challenges. There will be obstacles, resistance, and setbacks along the way. However, it is important to persevere and maintain a determined mindset. By staying focused on the goals and benefits of the Darwinian approach to management, leaders and employees can overcome these challenges and navigate the path to success.

Perseverance and determination are key components of resilience. Resilient leaders and employees can weather storms of change and continue to push forward, even in the face of adversity. They must maintain a positive outlook, remain adaptable, and keep their eyes fixed on the prize. To develop perseverance and determination, leaders and employees can practice the following strategies.

- **Setting achievable goals**. By breaking down large goals into smaller, more manageable steps, individuals can experience the satisfaction of meeting milestones along the way. This can help build momentum and motivation.

- **Celebrating progress**. Recognizing and celebrating progress, no matter how small, can help keep individuals motivated and focused on their goals.

- **Maintaining a positive mindset**. Focusing on the positive aspects of a situation and looking for opportunities to learn and grow can help maintain a positive outlook, even in the face of adversity.

- **Building resilience**. Engaging in activities and practices that build resilience, such as exercise, mindfulness, and self-care, can help individuals maintain their determination and perseverance.

9 THE FUTURE OF MANAGEMENT

If you implement the lessons from this book and find yourself at a point where you can look back on the journey to becoming an adaptive organization, take a moment to assess the challenges that have been overcome. This includes taking stock of the obstacles that were encountered and the strategies that were implemented to overcome them.

Think about the resistance to change that was encountered and the steps that were taken to address it. How was the plan of action developed and implemented, and what were the results? What were the biggest challenges and how were they overcome?

By reflecting on the challenges overcome, you can gain a deeper understanding of the obstacles that were encountered and the strategies that were effective in overcoming them. This will provide valuable insights that can be applied to future challenges and opportunities. Remember. adaptation is a continuous process, not an end-goal that can be reached. Keep changing.

- **Identifying areas of improvement**. As you reflect on the journey, it's important to identify areas of improvement. Take a critical look at what worked well and what could have been done differently. Think about the goals that were set and whether they were achieved. Were there any unexpected challenges or obstacles that arose? Could you have foreseen them? How could the plan of action have been improved to better address these challenges? By identifying areas of improvement, you can gain a deeper understanding of what worked well and what could be done differently in the future. This will help you continuously improve and become more effective in navigating the challenges and obstacles that arise in a rapidly changing business environment.

- **Celebrating successes and accomplishments.** Did you celebrate the successes and accomplishments along the way? Acknowledge the hard work and effort put in by everyone involved and the impact that was made. What were the key moments of success and what made them possible? How did everyone come together to achieve these successes? By celebrating the successes and accomplishments, you can boost morale and encourage continued progress. It also provides an opportunity to acknowledge the hard work and effort put in by everyone involved, which can help foster a sense of pride and ownership in the organization's success. In the next chapter, we will look more closely at different options to celebrate achievements.

- **Gaining new insights and lessons learned.** Are there any insights and lessons learned that can be applied to future endeavors? This includes taking a step back to understand the broader context of the journey and the impact that was made. Think about the strategies that were implemented and their impact. What did you learn about the business environment, the organization, and yourself? What insights and lessons can be applied to future challenges and opportunities? By gaining new insights and lessons learned, you can continually improve and become more effective in navigating the challenges and obstacles that arise in a rapidly changing business environment. It also provides an opportunity to share these insights and lessons with others, which can help build a culture of continuous learning and improvement.

- **Planning for the future and continual growth.** Look ahead and plan for the future. Set new goals to continue to grow and adapt. What are your goals for the future, and what steps will you take to achieve them. By planning for the future and continually growing and adapting, you can ensure that your organization stays ahead of the curve and continues to achieve success. It also provides a sense of direction and purpose, as you work towards a shared goal and vision for the future.

The potential future of the business world. The business world is constantly evolving, and it is essential for companies to adapt to keep up with changes. The future of management holds many possibilities, and Darwinian organizations that are agile and resilient are well-positioned to succeed. Some potential trends in the business world include:

- **Increased digitization and automation**. As technology continues to advance, more tasks will be automated, leading to changes in the workforce and the way companies operate.

- **Greater emphasis on sustainability and social responsibility**. Companies will be expected to operate in a manner that is not only profitable but also environmentally and socially responsible.

- **More diverse and inclusive workplace**. The business world is becoming increasingly diverse, and companies will need to embrace diversity and inclusivity to attract and retain talent.

- **Focus on employee well-being**. Companies will place a greater emphasis on the well-being of employees, including work-life balance, mental health, and physical health.

- **Emergence of new industries and markets**. With technological advancements and changing consumer needs, new industries and markets will emerge, presenting opportunities for companies to innovate and grow.

By embracing the principles of the Darwinian approach to management, organizations can prepare themselves to navigate these changes and take advantage of new opportunities. They will be equipped to lead with resilience, evaluate and improve performance, and navigate the challenges of change with perseverance and determination.

The role of the Darwinian approach to management in shaping the future. As the business world continues to evolve, the Darwinian approach to management is poised to play an increasingly important role in shaping its future. This approach emphasizes the importance of continuous adaptation and improvement, which are essential for organizations to remain competitive and succeed in an ever-changing business landscape.

Adopting a Darwinian approach to management requires a shift in mindset from a focus on stability and control to a focus on flexibility and growth. This means embracing experimentation, failure, and constant adaptation to ensure that organizations are always improving and staying ahead of the curve.

By embracing this approach, organizations can build a culture of innovation and creativity, where employees are empowered to take risks and continuously improve their processes and systems. This can lead to greater efficiency, effectiveness, and overall success in a rapidly changing business environment.

Additionally, the Darwinian approach to management helps organizations to stay agile and responsive to change, making it easier to pivot and adapt when necessary. This is particularly important in an age where technology and market conditions are constantly shifting and evolving, requiring organizations to be able to adapt quickly to stay ahead.

The Darwinian approach to management offers a roadmap for organizations looking to succeed in the future of business. By embracing this approach, organizations can build a culture of continuous improvement, become more agile and responsive to change, and position themselves for long-term success.

Preparing for and embracing the future. As the business world continues to evolve and change, organizations need to be prepared for what the future may hold. By embracing the Darwinian approach to management, organizations can position themselves to be at the forefront of the changes that are to come.

One way to prepare for the future is to constantly be learning and adapting. By staying informed on the latest trends, technologies, and best practices, organizations can ensure they are always moving in the right direction.

Another important aspect of preparing for the future is to invest in talent development. Organizations that are proactive in developing the skills and abilities of their employees will be better equipped to navigate the challenges and opportunities that lie ahead.

Finally, organizations must have a culture of continuous improvement. By constantly looking for ways to improve processes, systems, and practices, organizations can stay ahead of the curve and be ready for whatever the future may bring.

By embracing the future with an open mind, a willingness to learn and adapt, and a culture of continuous improvement, organizations can ensure they are well-positioned to succeed in a rapidly changing business world.

10 CELEBRATING VICTORY:
BUILDING A CULTURE OF COLLABORATION

Envision a time when you have successfully navigated the challenges and obstacles of implementing the Darwinian approach to management in your company and the hard work and determination have paid off. Your company or department is now thriving and setting a new standard in the industry.

At this time, it is crucial to acknowledge and celebrate success. This is not only a way to recognize the efforts of your team, but it also provides an opportunity to reflect on the journey and the personal growth and development that has taken place.

When planning your celebration, consider gathering your team together to acknowledge their contributions and hard work. This can be a simple gesture, such as a team lunch, or a more elaborate event. The important thing is to show appreciation for the team's efforts and to celebrate the success together.

In this moment of triumph, take a deep breath and soak in the satisfaction of a job well done. The journey has been challenging, but the reward is worth it. Congratulate yourself and your team on a job well done.

Recognizing the contributions of the team. One of the key factors in the success of your company is the hard work and dedication of your team. It's important to acknowledge and recognize the efforts of each team member to maintain a positive and motivated work environment. When recognizing the contributions of your team, consider the following.

- Acknowledge the individual contributions of each team member.
- Highlight the team's collective efforts and the impact they have had on the company's success.
- Provide opportunities for team members to share their experiences and insights.
- Show appreciation for the team's hard work and dedication.

This can be done in various ways, such as through a formal award ceremony, a team celebration, or through individual recognition and rewards. The important thing is to acknowledge and recognize the efforts of each team member and to show appreciation for their contributions.

By recognizing the contributions of your team, you will not only boost morale, but also foster a culture of collaboration and teamwork. This, in turn, will contribute to the ongoing success of your company.

Celebrating accomplishments. Celebrating your company's success is an important step in recognizing the hard work and dedication of your team. It's a way to acknowledge the achievements of the company and to show appreciation for the efforts of each team member. When planning your celebration, consider the following.

- Make it a team event. Celebrating as a team creates a sense of unity and reinforces the importance of teamwork in the success of the company.
- Choose a venue that is appropriate for your team and the occasion. This could be a restaurant, a park, or another location that is fitting for the celebration.
- Plan activities that are enjoyable for everyone. Consider activities that will engage and entertain your team, such as games, activities, or a team lunch.

- Show appreciation for the team's efforts. Acknowledge the hard work and dedication of each team member through individual recognition and rewards.

Celebrating the accomplishments of your company is an opportunity to reflect on the journey, to acknowledge the contributions of each team member, and to show appreciation for their hard work. It's a time to come together as a team, to have fun, and to celebrate the success of the company. By taking the time to celebrate your company's accomplishments, you will reinforce the importance of teamwork and collaboration, and you will contribute to the ongoing success of your company.

Reflecting on the journey. Implementing the Darwinian approach to management will have been a journey of discovery and growth for the team. It's important to take a moment to reflect on the journey and to acknowledge the personal growth and development that has taken place. When reflecting on the journey, consider the following.

- Reflect on the challenges and obstacles faced and how they were overcome.
- Acknowledge the personal growth and development that has taken place.
- Consider the impact of the Darwinian approach to management on the company and its employees.
- Reflect on the lessons learned and the ways in which they can be applied in the future.
- Reflecting on the journey is an opportunity to gain insight into the challenges and obstacles faced, and to acknowledge the personal growth and development that has taken place. It's a time to reflect on the lessons learned and to consider the impact of the Darwinian approach to management on the company and its employees.

By taking the time to reflect on the journey, the team will gain a deeper understanding of the challenges and obstacles faced, and they will be better prepared to navigate future challenges. This, in turn, will contribute to the ongoing success of the company.

Looking to the future. The successful implementation of the Darwinian approach to management will have positioned the reader's company for continued adaptation, success and growth. When looking to the future, consider the following.

- Assess the current state of the company and identify areas for improvement.

- Consider potential growth opportunities and the ways in which they can be pursued.

- Develop a plan for ongoing improvement and growth.

- Encourage continued personal growth and development for the reader and their team.

Looking to the future is an opportunity to assess the current state of the company and to identify areas for improvement. It's a time to consider potential growth opportunities and to develop a plan for ongoing improvement and growth.

By taking a proactive approach to the future, the reader and their team will be better equipped to navigate challenges and obstacles, and they will be positioned for continued success and growth. The Darwinian approach to management provides a foundation for ongoing success, and by looking to the future, the reader and their team can ensure the continued success of their company.

Building a culture of collaboration and teamwork. Collaboration is a critical component of success in any organization, and in a rapidly changing business environment, it is more important than ever. The key to building a culture of collaboration is creating a shared sense of purpose and fostering open and effective communication.

One effective way to build a culture of collaboration is to encourage teamwork across departments. This can be achieved through the creation of cross-functional teams, the formation of partnerships between departments, and the sharing of resources and information.

It is also important to foster a culture of trust, where employees feel comfortable sharing their ideas and opinions, and where they know that their contributions are valued. This can be achieved through regular team-building activities, open forums for discussion and feedback, and by recognizing and rewarding collaboration and teamwork.

Finally, it is important to establish clear and consistent guidelines for collaboration, including expectations for communication, decision-making processes, and problem-solving methods. By establishing these guidelines, organizations can ensure that collaboration is effective and efficient, and that everyone is working together to achieve common goals.

- **Overcoming interdepartmental silos and fostering interdepartmental cooperation**. To build a culture of collaboration and teamwork, it is crucial to overcome the interdepartmental silos that often exist within organizations. These silos can create a divide between departments and prevent effective collaboration, leading to inefficiencies and missed opportunities. To overcome these silos, leaders must foster a culture of open communication, trust, and mutual respect between departments. This can be done through.

- **Regular interdepartmental meetings**. Scheduling regular meetings between departments can help to break down silos and encourage communication and cooperation. During these meetings, departments can discuss their goals and challenges, and explore opportunities for collaboration.

- **Joint projects and initiatives**. Encouraging departments to work together on joint projects and initiatives can help to build a culture of collaboration. By working together on a common goal, departments can develop a deeper understanding of each other's strengths and weaknesses and learn how to better support one another.

- **Cross-training opportunities**. Providing cross-training opportunities for employees can help to break down silos and encourage interdepartmental cooperation. When employees have a better understanding of what their colleagues do and how their work fits into the overall organization, they are more likely to collaborate effectively.

- **Celebrating success together.** Celebrating success as an organization, rather than as separate departments, can help to foster a culture of collaboration. By recognizing the contributions of all departments, leaders can help to build a sense of teamwork and shared purpose.

The importance of cross-functional collaboration in achieving success. Collaboration between departments is a critical aspect of building a successful adaptive organization. Silos can often arise within an organization due to differing goals, responsibilities, and ways of working. These silos can limit the flow of ideas, hinder progress and ultimately hinder success.

Fostering interdepartmental cooperation requires leadership to be proactive in breaking down these barriers. Leaders must encourage open communication, create opportunities for cross-functional collaboration, and support a culture of teamwork. Regular team-building exercises, cross-functional projects, and open forums for discussion can help to foster a culture of collaboration.

Cross-functional collaboration is also essential for achieving success in a rapidly changing business environment. By bringing together individuals with different skills and perspectives, organizations can identify and solve problems in innovative ways. This type of collaboration also fosters a deeper understanding of each department's responsibilities, goals, and challenges, helping to build trust and create a more cohesive organization.

Building a culture of collaboration is an essential aspect of the Darwinian approach to management. By overcoming interdepartmental silos and fostering cross-functional collaboration, organizations can achieve success in a rapidly changing business environment. By working together, teams can identify new opportunities, solve problems in innovative ways, and achieve success through collective effort.

11 REFLECTIONS ON THE JOURNEY AND LESSONS LEARNED

It's been quite a journey so far, hasn't it? When we first set out on this adventure, you were called to action to embrace a new way of doing things. You were faced with resistance from those who were comfortable with the old ways of doing business, but hopefully you persevered. With the guidance of a new theory of management, you stepped out of your comfort zone and navigated obstacles to build alliances and make important decisions. You proved the value of the adaptive approach and ultimately achieved success.

As we reflect on all that has been accomplished, remember the key moments of growth and the lessons we've learned along the way. From overcoming resistance to change, to proving the value of the adaptive approach, you've come a long way. Now, it's time to share what you've learned with others.

Key takeaways from the Darwinian approach to management. First and foremost, we've learned the importance of being adaptable in a rapidly changing business environment. We've seen the value of having a good theory to guide us, and the benefits of stepping out of our comfort zone. We've experienced the power of building alliances and working together, and the crucial role of making informed decisions. And, of course, we've seen the rewards of persevering through challenges to achieve success.

Take a moment to reflect on these key steppingstones and consider how you can apply them in your own organization. The adaptive approach to management has proven to be a successful method for navigating the challenges of the business world and leading your organization to success. These takeaways are crucial for any leader who wants to stay ahead in today's rapidly changing business environment.

The Impact of the Darwinian Approach on the Corporation. What improvements have we seen in efficiency, productivity, and overall success? And what cultural changes have taken place within the organization because of our new approach?

First, let's look at the impact on the bottom line. The Darwinian approach has been shown to increase efficiency and productivity, leading to improved success for the corporation. But the impact goes beyond just numbers - it also touches the people within the organization.

The adaptive approach can foster a sense of empowerment and collaboration, as well as a culture of continuous improvement. These cultural changes can have a lasting impact on the success and sustainability of the corporation.

Take a moment to consider the impact of the Darwinian approach in your own organization. How has it affected the bottom line and the people within your corporation? And don't keep these lessons to yourself - share them with others and help spread the word about the benefits of the adaptive approach.

Sharing the Lessons Learned with Others. As we come to the end of our journey, we must not forget the importance of sharing the lessons learned with others. We've learned so much along the way - from the key takeaways of the adaptive approach to management, to the impact it has had on our corporation, to the lessons learned from overcoming challenges and achieving success. And it would be a shame to keep all of this knowledge to ourselves.

Sharing our experiences and lessons learned is a crucial step in the process of continuous improvement and growth. By spreading the word about the adaptive approach and its benefits, we can help others to achieve success in their own organizations.

So, make a point to share your experiences and lessons learned with others. This could be through formal presentations, mentoring relationships, or simply through casual conversations with colleagues. By sharing what we've learned, we can help others to embark on their own journeys of growth and improvement.

Reflections on Personal Growth and the Future of the Adaptive Organization. Think about the skills and knowledge you've gained along the way. Consider your vision for the future of the adaptive approach. And don't forget to consider the potential for continued growth and improvement, both for yourself and for the organization.

The future of the adaptive organization is bright, if we continue to embrace the principles of adaptability and evolution that have brought us this far. By reflecting on our personal growth and the future of the adaptive approach, we can ensure that we are well-equipped to continue leading the way towards a brighter future for all.

Take a moment to reflect on your own personal growth and the future of the adaptive organization. By doing so, you'll be well-positioned to continue driving progress and success for years to come.

The Importance of Effective Decision-Making in Times of Change. Change is a constant in the business world, and the ability to make effective decisions is critical to navigating the challenges and obstacles that come with it. Whether it's responding to market changes, adapting to new technologies, or navigating shifting customer needs, the ability to make critical decisions is essential to achieving success in a rapidly changing business environment.

Effective decision-making requires a combination of careful analysis, clear communication, and a willingness to embrace risk. It requires a deep understanding of the situation, the ability to weigh options and trade-offs, and the courage to act in the face of uncertainty.

One of the key challenges of decision-making in times of change is managing the tension between short-term and long-term goals. On one hand, the need to respond quickly to changing circumstances may require a focus on short-term results. On the other hand, the importance of building a sustainable and resilient organization for the future requires a focus on long-term outcomes.

Balancing these conflicting priorities requires a clear understanding of the organization's values and mission, and a commitment to making decisions that align with these core principles. It also requires a willingness to embrace change and a continuous learning mindset, always seeking new insights and perspectives that can inform better decision-making.

In the end, the ability to make effective decisions in times of change is what sets the adaptive organizations apart from those that are left behind. With a commitment to continuous learning, a focus on core values, and a willingness to embrace risk and uncertainty, organizations can navigate the challenges of change and achieve long-term success.

Balancing Short-Term and Long-Term Goals. In a rapidly changing business environment, leaders are often faced with the challenge of balancing short-term and long-term goals. On one hand, there is a need to address immediate challenges and make decisions that will help the organization survive in the short-term. On the other hand, it is important to make decisions that will set the organization up for success in the long-term. Navigating this tension is a critical aspect of effective decision-making.

One approach to balancing short-term and long-term goals is to prioritize and allocate resources in a way that supports both. For example, an organization may choose to invest in short-term initiatives that will help it weather current challenges, while also investing in long-term initiatives that will position it for future success. This requires a strategic and well-informed approach to decision-making, as well as a willingness to prioritize and allocate resources in a way that supports both short-term and long-term goals.

Another key factor in balancing short-term and long-term goals is the ability to effectively manage risk. In a rapidly changing business environment, it is important to be able to identify and mitigate risks, while also making decisions that will allow the organization to take advantage of new opportunities. This requires leaders to have a deep understanding of the risks and opportunities that are present in the business environment, as well as the ability to make informed and strategic decisions.

Ultimately, the key to balancing short-term and long-term goals is the ability to effectively navigate the tension between the two. This requires leaders to have a clear understanding of both the challenges and opportunities that are present in the business environment, as well as the ability to make informed and strategic decisions that will help the organization achieve success in the short-term and long-term.

Navigating the Tension of Change and Making Decisions in the Best Interest of the Organization. As a leader, making decisions is one of the most challenging parts of the job. This is especially true in times of change when uncertainty and conflicting priorities can create a high level of tension. To navigate this tension and make decisions that are in the best interest of the organization, it's important to approach decision-making with a clear and strategic mindset.

One effective strategy for balancing short-term and long-term goals is to take a step back and consider the bigger picture. Ask yourself what the organization needs in order to be successful in the long run, and then align your decisions with those goals. This doesn't mean ignoring short-term needs, but it does mean prioritizing the long-term health of the organization over immediate gains.

Another strategy is to involve key stakeholders in the decision-making process. This can help you understand different perspectives and get buy-in for your decisions. In addition, involving stakeholders can help you make better decisions by incorporating a range of viewpoints and insights.

Finally, it's important to be open and transparent about the decision-making process. This means being transparent about the reasoning behind your decisions, as well as the outcomes you hope to achieve. This can help build trust and create a sense of accountability, which is crucial in times of change.

In conclusion, making critical decisions in times of change can be challenging, but it's essential for the success of the organization. By balancing short-term and long-term goals, involving key stakeholders, and being transparent about the decision-making process, you can navigate the tension of change and make decisions that are in the best interest of the organization.

The Darwinian approach to management has numerous benefits for organizations facing challenges in a rapidly changing business environment. By embracing the principles of natural selection and adapting to change, organizations can achieve success and thrive in the face of uncertainty.

One key aspect of the Darwinian approach is the development of a culture of experimentation and risk-taking. By encouraging creativity and innovation, organizations are better equipped to stay ahead of the curve and adapt to changes in the market. This fosters a dynamic and agile organization that can respond to new opportunities and challenges.

Another benefit of the Darwinian approach is the development of a resilient organization. By embracing a growth mindset and building a culture of continuous learning, organizations can develop the skills and resources necessary to overcome obstacles and navigate challenges. This not only improves the ability of the organization to adapt to change, but also increases its ability to withstand uncertainty and volatility in the business environment.

Finally, the Darwinian approach encourages cross-functional collaboration and teamwork. By fostering interdepartmental cooperation, organizations can better leverage their collective strengths and resources, improving their ability to achieve success and navigate change. Remember that cooperation is the human superpower.

In summary, the Darwinian approach to management offers organizations numerous benefits in a rapidly changing business environment. By embracing the principles of natural selection and adapting to change, organizations can achieve success and thrive in the face of uncertainty. Remember these points:

- Evolutionary principles can be applied to the business world to increase adaptability and resilience.

- Overcoming resistance to change is crucial for the success of a Darwinian approach.
- Building an adaptive culture is essential for fostering a culture of change and evolution.
- Embracing experimentation and failure is important for growth and success.
- Resilience is crucial for leaders and employees to navigate change and adversity.
- Performance should be evaluated and improved by tracking progress and using data.
- Navigating the challenges of change requires perseverance and determination.
- Preparing for and embracing the future is essential for continued growth and success.

A final word of encouragement for those embarking on the journey to build an adaptive organization. As you reach the end of this book, you may feel a sense of uncertainty about the challenges ahead. How do the insights from this book apply to your situation? Building an adaptive organization is not an easy task, but it is one that can bring immense rewards for your company and for you as a leader.

Remember the key insights and lessons learned, including the importance of embracing a Darwinian approach to management, overcoming resistance to change, fostering an adaptive culture, embracing experimentation and failure, leading with resilience, and continuously evaluating and improving performance.

Most importantly, don't forget the importance of perseverance and determination in the face of adversity. The journey to building an adaptive organization is not easy, but with hard work and determination, you can overcome the obstacles and succeed. Don't fear change.

Believe in yourself, believe in your team, and believe in the power of evolution. For those who embrace change and take an adaptive approach to management, the future is bright.

12 TEN KEY TAKEAWAYS

1. **Darwinian management**. The book introduces Darwinian principles and how they apply to business, with a focus on the principle of natural selection and how it relates to organizational development. Darwinian principles refer to the ideas and theories developed by the British naturalist Charles Darwin, particularly his theory of evolution through natural selection. These principles state that species evolve and change over time through a process of natural selection, where individuals with advantageous traits are more likely to survive and pass on their traits to their offspring. In the context of business, Darwinian principles can be applied to organizational change, where companies must adapt and evolve to survive and succeed. The key idea is that organizations that can better adapt to their business environment are more likely to survive and thrive, just as individuals that are better adapted to their environment are more likely to survive and reproduce.

2. **Adaptation and resilience**. The book emphasizes the importance of adaptation and resilience in the business world, highlighting how

organizations can become more adaptable and better equipped to thrive in a rapidly changing environment.

- *Adaptation* refers to the ability of a system or organism to change or adjust in response to new or changing circumstances. In the context of management and business, adaptation refers to the ability of a company to change and adjust in response to changes in the market, technology, or other external factors. It involves developing the capacity to quickly respond to new challenges and opportunities.

- *Resilience*, on the other hand, refers to the ability of a system or organism to withstand stress, adversity, or change, and to recover quickly from disruptions. In the context of management and business, resilience refers to the ability of a company to remain effective and stable in the face of challenges, such as market changes, economic downturns, or other disruptions. It involves developing the capacity to absorb and adapt to changes, as well as the ability to bounce back from setbacks and recover from disruptions.

3. **Overcome resistance to change**. The book addresses the challenges of navigating resistance to change within the organization, including how to address objections and misconceptions about the Darwinian approach to management and build buy-in and support. Overcoming resistance to change refers to the process of managing and mitigating objections, fears, and concerns that arise when an organization introduces a new approach or initiative. When a company decides to implement a new approach, such as a Darwinian approach to management, there may be individuals or groups within the organization who are resistant to change. This resistance may stem from issues such as a lack of understanding of the new approach, concerns about job security, or a general discomfort with the unknown. To overcome resistance to change, leaders must identify and understand the sources of resistance. This involves gathering input from employees and other stakeholders to identify their concerns.

Leaders can then address these objections head-on, providing clear and concise explanations of the benefits of the new approach and how it will benefit the organization. They can also involve employees in the process of change, giving them a sense of ownership and responsibility in the transition. Additionally, building buy-in and support from key stakeholders is crucial in overcoming resistance to change. This may involve creating a sense of urgency or demonstrating the need for change, as well as involving stakeholders in the decision-making process and communicating the benefits of the new approach. By overcoming resistance to change, leaders can ensure that their organization is better equipped to navigate challenges and obstacles and ultimately achieve success in a rapidly changing business environment.

4. **Use scientific management practices.** The theory of evolution explains how species change over time through natural selection and sexual selection, which are the mechanisms by which certain traits become more prevalent in a population over time. Natural selection favors traits that provide a survival advantage, while sexual selection favors traits that enhance an individual's ability to attract or compete for mates. In business management, the concepts of evolution, natural selection, and sexual selection can be applied to continuously adapt and evolve to changing conditions, pass on organizational culture and knowledge, and select ideas, products, and employees that align with the organization's goals and needs. Variation plays a crucial role in evolution and adaptation, providing the raw material for selection to act upon, while adaptation is the key factor in the survival and evolution of species and the process of adjusting and modifying products, organizational practices, processes, and structures in response to changes in the internal and external environment.

5. **Navigate challenges and obstacles.** The book provides practical strategies and tactics for overcoming the challenges and obstacles that organizations face in implementing the Darwinian approach to

management. Navigating challenges and obstacles refers to the process of overcoming difficulties that arise during the implementation of a new approach or change in an organization. In this context, it refers to the difficulties that may be encountered when implementing a Darwinian approach to management within a corporation. Some examples of challenges and obstacles include resistance from employees who are comfortable with the old ways of doing business, navigating objections and misconceptions about the new approach, and overcoming the technical difficulties of implementing a new system. To successfully navigate these challenges and obstacles, it is important to have a resilient organization that can adapt and thrive in a rapidly changing environment, a culture of collaboration and teamwork, and effective decision-making that balances short-term and long-term goals.

6. **Market awareness**. The book highlights the importance of market awareness and adapting to market changes to stay ahead of the curve and navigate uncertainty and change in the business world. Market awareness refers to the ability of an organization to understand and keep track of the changes and trends in the market. This means having a clear understanding of the current market conditions, customer needs and preferences, as well as the competition and market trends. It involves paying attention to the market signals and adapting to market changes in a timely manner. Market awareness is important for organizations because it helps them to stay ahead of the curve and make informed business decisions that will help them succeed in a rapidly changing business environment. By having a good understanding of the market, organizations can identify opportunities for growth, and make strategic moves that will help them remain competitive and relevant.

7. **Embrace a growth mindset by encouraging creativity and risk-taking**. The book emphasizes the importance of embracing a growth mindset and developing a culture of experimentation and risk-taking to

lead the organization towards success. Embracing a growth mindset refers to a mentality that sees challenges and failures as opportunities for learning and growth, rather than as permanent setbacks. It is about adopting a positive, proactive approach to life and work, recognizing that skills and abilities can be developed through effort and practice. When applied to the business world, embracing a growth mindset can help leaders and employees to be more open to new ideas, take calculated risks, and continuously learn and adapt in the face of changing market conditions. By embracing a growth mindset, organizations can foster a culture of innovation, experimentation, and continuous improvement. However, encouraging creativity and risk-taking often requires a shift in organizational culture and a willingness to embrace change. Remember to celebrate both failures and successes, as both indicate that experimentation and learning are taking place. Develop a supportive environment that encourages employees to experiment, take risks, and continuously learn and grow. By embracing creativity and risk-taking, organizations can build a culture that supports innovation and is better equipped to adapt to changing market conditions.

8. **Build a culture of collaboration.** The book emphasizes the importance of building a culture of collaboration and overcoming interdepartmental silos to foster interdepartmental cooperation. This creates a work environment where employees feel supported, valued, and encouraged to work together. It is a company-wide mindset that prioritizes teamwork, open communication, and the sharing of knowledge and resources. A culture of collaboration fosters trust, inclusiveness, and a sense of belonging among employees, leading to improved productivity, increased innovation, and better overall performance. To build a culture of collaboration, organizations should promote open communication channels, provide opportunities for team-building activities, and recognize and reward team successes. Additionally, leaders must set the tone by modeling collaborative behavior and providing regular feedback to employees on how they can

improve their teamwork skills. A culture of collaboration requires a long-term commitment from everyone in the organization, but the benefits are well worth the effort.

9. **Effective decision-making**. The book highlights the importance of effective decision-making in times of change, including how to balance short-term and long-term goals and navigate the tension of change. Effective decision-making is the process of making well-informed, thought-out choices that bring the best possible outcome. It involves gathering and analyzing information, considering options, deciding, and taking action. The key to effective decision-making is to approach the process in a systematic and logical manner. Some of the key concepts in effective decision-making include.

   - **Define the problem or opportunity**. Clearly stating the problem or opportunity is the first step in the decision-making process.
   - **Gather information**. Gather as much relevant information as possible to help inform your decision. This could involve research, talking to experts, or consulting with others.
   - **Weigh options**. Once you have the information you need, consider all possible options for resolving the problem or taking advantage of the opportunity.
   - **Make the decision**. Choose the best option based on the information you have gathered and the criteria you have set.
   - **Act**. Implement the decision by taking the necessary steps to bring it to fruition.
   - **Evaluate the outcome**. After the decision has been implemented, assess the outcome, and make any necessary changes. This helps to improve decision-making in the future.

10. **Continuous learning and adaptation**. The book stresses the importance of continuous learning and adaptation in the business world. It highlights the benefits of the Darwinian approach to management for achieving success in a rapidly changing environment.

Continuous learning and adaptation refer to the ongoing process of acquiring new knowledge, skills, and experiences to continuously improve and adapt to changing circumstances and environments. In today's rapidly changing world, it's essential to have a growth mindset and be open to new ideas and opportunities to stay ahead and succeed. Effective continuous learning involves regularly seeking out new information and experiences, being open to feedback, and being proactive in seeking out new challenges to improve one's skills and knowledge. Organizations that encourage and support continuous learning and adaptation tend to be more agile, innovative, and successful. By investing in the development of their employees, organizations can foster a culture of continuous improvement and ensure their employees are equipped with the skills and knowledge necessary to meet the demands of an ever-changing business landscape. Additionally, continuous learning and adaptation is a key component of personal growth and development, allowing individuals to build a fulfilling and meaningful career.

Darwinian principles have been at work for millions of years and resulted in the rich diversity of life we see today. II you know how; you can make these principles work for you. Best of luck with your future endeavors.

ABOUT THE AUTHOR

The author has been a researcher of evolutionary biology for 25 years.
Here, writing under pseudonym.